SONGS FROM A WINDOW

END-OF-LIFE STORIES FROM THE MUSIC THERAPY ROOM

BOB HEATH

In memory of Alan MacGregor 1944–2017

CONTENTS

NEIL

LYRICS

FOREWORD

I've been a musician all of my life and, for the last twenty years or so, I've worked as a music therapist, predominantly with people who are struggling to cope with loss in one way or another. Loss is so often at the heart of our human encounters, whether we are therapists, doctors, nurses, teachers, managers, parents…friends. We will all at some stage face the challenge of being alongside someone who's grieving the loss of something, or somebody. And for almost all of us, the greatest of these losses and the hardest one to face will be death. We'll do pretty well anything we can to avoid talking about it, or even thinking about it. We'll gladly hand over our money to research organisations who work tirelessly to find cures for the very things that threaten to take our lives from us. And we'll dip into our pockets again to support the amazing organisations who provide care and comfort for those of us for whom the cures will come too late. And that's most of us—all of us in fact. One way or another, we are all going to die, and dying is never going to be easy.

Shortly after I started writing this book, I was diagnosed with bowel cancer. I was lucky; it was stage 2 and the doctors were able to operate very quickly and remove the tumour. However, a couple of weeks after the surgery, I became extremely unwell and was rushed back into hospital, where I was treated for sepsis. At one point I woke to find my consultant sitting in a chair at my bedside with his head in his hands. He looked up at me and apologised.

'I'm sorry,' he said. 'I just don't know how this could have happened.'

My immediate thought was, *Oh, my God, is he trying to tell me I'm going to die? Well, I'm* definitely *not going to have* that *conversation, that's for sure.* So I responded with, 'You look very tired, doctor. When was the last time you had a proper rest?'

He began to tell me about his family, his newly born daughter and the pressures at home, particularly when no one was getting much sleep. I listened sympathetically and gently reminded him about the importance of taking care of himself. Eventually he checked my drip, looked at my charts and left me with a weary nod and a smile. I still didn't know how ill I was, and that was the point—I'd successfully avoided having to talk about anything that might even hint at my own mortality.

Twenty years in end-of-life care, hundreds of clients, and just look at you, I thought to myself rather scornfully. *What* have *you learnt*?

This book will introduce you to a few of the clients I've worked with over the last twenty years. It's stories of my encounters with some extraordinary people at an extraordinary time in their lives. Some of these encounters are very brief, others not so. In the interests of confidentiality, I've changed the clients' names, along with many of the places and other details, but their stories are still true. It is, in part, a book about living and dying and music therapy but, in writing the stories, I've come to realise that it's mostly a book about relationships, the human spirit, hope and love.

I learnt very early on in my career as a therapist that the devil was in the detail and that I needed to balance the temptation to unpick my clients' life stories forensically, with the need to simply be alongside and support them in what would almost always be the last few months of their lives. This became my overriding philosophy as I began to write these stories; they're less about everything my clients told me, and more about what I really heard and received, and how we, together in the music room, assimilated it.

A few years ago at a conference, I was introduced by a highly esteemed consultant who described me as having the best and the worst job in palliative care. 'The best,' he said, 'because he's got music, and with music you can get to very deep places with patients, very quickly. And the worst, because sometimes it's an absolute bugger trying to get back out again.'

We all know about the power of music, don't we? It's written into all of our lives; regardless of what we profess to love or hate, music sits at the very heart of being human; it always has. It's surely no accident that the world is full of songs. They identify us as individuals and define our groups; they help us celebrate our victories and mourn our losses; they capture our history and secure it for generations to come. We form deep associations with songs that other people have written; their words become our words; we cherish them, nurture them and keep them in our hearts forever.

The songwriting process itself can be quite an emotional adventure; it's highly unpredictable and often very mysterious. Melodies, words or phrases can appear as if from nowhere, surprising us, revealing things that we hadn't anticipated (or, indeed, thought we'd known). In collaborative, creative relationships, therapists will need to become fellow adventurers, helping their clients to trust and develop the process to express and understand what they're feeling. This mutuality —the co-creation of care, if you like—is an essential ingredient in an authentic, genuine, therapeutic relationship. And, as Irvin Yalom, the great therapist and teacher, often reminds us, by facilitating change in their clients, the therapists themselves become changed. Working as a music therapist in palliative care has changed me in all sorts of ways and in some, I'm sure, that I've yet to recognise.

Everyone I've met has had an amazing back story and that's because *we all do*. Regardless of who we are or where we're from, we all live with the duality of being human. We are all known and we are all unknown. Perhaps it's at the end of our lives, when there's only one outcome that we're absolutely sure of—faced with the great existential challenge of dying—that the two can begin to become one. It's a matter of the soul and the shadow, isn't it? Like words, and music.

JONATHAN

SKINNY GHOST

I don't know where you are, and until I do,
I will watch my pace, I will wait for grace, and I will hold this
space for you.
'Skinny Ghost', Bob Heath

I became a music therapist fairly late in my working life, although I've been a musician and songwriter ever since I could hold an instrument and get some sort of tune out of it. In my twenties I spent equal amounts of time engaging with and avoiding the music business. I loved writing, recording and performing but I never felt particularly comfortable with the music industry itself. I knew that something was missing but for a long time I struggled to identify what that was. Through a combination of sheer good fortune and the kindness and belief of close friends, I eventually found myself working as a community musician and began to learn how to make music all over again—this time with profoundly disabled young people.

It was during one of my early sessions in a special school that I first met Jonathan. He was seventeen years old and had been diagnosed as profoundly autistic. I can remember this meeting vividly because, despite my many attempts to communicate with him, he refused to engage with me in any way, preferring to lower his head and cast his eyes towards his feet, his face a picture of boredom and contempt. This had been my first experience of rejection in my new role as a workshop leader and I left the session feeling rattled, fraudulent and summarily dismissed. Jonathan, I thought to myself as I drove home, really hadn't liked me at all.

It therefore came as quite a shock when a few days later someone called me and said, 'I'm Jonathan's mother. You met him at school a few days ago and we think something quite interesting might have happened.'

'Mmm, well,' I said. 'Thank you, but I think he felt I was pretty useless to be quite honest.'

'On the contrary, my dear,' she replied. 'He thought you were rather fascinating and he wants to meet you again, very soon please, here at home.' I was far from convinced that this was a good idea but saying 'no' was clearly not going to be an option.

Home was a beautiful farmhouse in Berkshire, complete with an entire annexe which had been converted for Jonathan. As I negotiated the long drive through the farm grounds for the first time, I was still feeling rather bewildered by the request for my presence and, frankly, terrified at the prospect of meeting Jonathan again, and for that matter, his mother, Joan, who I was convinced was in for something of a disappointment. Joan led me into the kitchen where we sat at the huge farmhouse table and she offered me some tea.

'Jonny will be with us in a minute,' she said. 'He's very excited; he's been telling me all about you.'

My heart was sinking fast. The Jonathan I'd met didn't speak; in fact Jonathan *couldn't* speak—at all—and he certainly hadn't seemed very excited by me in the classroom. But I wasn't about to argue with Joan. She was a tall woman in her late sixties with eyes that looked straight into your heart and dismissed any notion you may have had of hiding. In Joan's formidable gaze, you were completely revealed.

'Now then,' she said, 'I've only just returned from a little trekking trip in the Himalayas and I'm so thrilled to hear Jonathan's news. He's been needing to meet someone like you for a long time and we're so delighted that it's finally happened.'

I decided to take a leap of faith. 'Does Jonathan talk to you?' I asked.

'Well of course he does, my dear. I'm his mother. He's always talked to me. Oh, not in the way that many people think their sons talk to them, but talk to me he does, in his own way, and I can hear him. Of course!'

'What has he told you about me?'

'Well, that he thinks you can help him to come to terms with some of the things that are frightening him.'

'What is he frightened of?' I asked.

'Well. Living, my dear, living and not dying.'

I took a breath or two and sat quietly for a few moments. 'Why does Jonathan think I can help him?' I wondered aloud. I was trying to sound calm and in control but in truth I was beginning to feel hopelessly insecure.

'Because Jonny knows these things about people; always has, dear.'

I sipped my tea, took another breath and asked gingerly, 'Then why do you think he was so openly dismissive of me at school last week?'

Joan placed her hand on top of mine and smiled. 'Oh that! Oh! He does that all the time. He's tough, you know, especially if he doesn't think you're the real thing. But sometimes he does it to test you; it's how he gets you to remember him.' She giggled and smiled at me.

'Okay then. Shall we go and see if he's ready?'

Throughout that late summer and autumn, I visited Jonathan regularly. Our music sessions were always preceded by tea with Joan, who would help me to piece together the story of Jonathan's life: a young bright man trapped inside a body that simply couldn't hold him. I began to see glimpses of him during our music sessions, particularly when I was singing songs that we just made up in the moment. Jonathan couldn't make any verbal contribution but somehow this didn't seem to matter. I sang about what I saw and what I felt, and being with Jonathan made it feel easy to sing for both of us.

I would check things out with him and he would shake his head from side to side excitedly while fixing me with a stare not unlike his mother's. He never smiled at me but from our first session, a bond between us had begun to develop and my fear of being rejected by him was soon replaced by something much more exciting. I began to look forward to our sessions and felt very alive and full of energy when we were together. Looking back, I don't think I ever really knew what I was doing but I knew that I wanted to be there.

'You must become a *professional* music therapist, my dear.' It was late in October and Joan had been listening in to our session from the next room. 'And Jonathan agrees.'

The truth was that I'd already decided to train as a music therapist and had managed to get a place on the course at Bristol University. Working with Jonathan had certainly influenced my thinking and I was looking forward to studying and exploring some of the mysteries that seemed to be present when we made music together.

'Jonny is delighted for you,' said Joan. 'We all are.'

On the day before I began training, I saw Jonathan at home for our regular session. He was more animated than I'd ever seen him, rocking in his chair, making fists with his hands and punching the air as he played the Soundbeam, an ultrasonic device that enables people to create musical sound by making movements inside a beam. I'd started singing 'All Along the Watchtower' and it felt as if Jonathan was prompting me from his chair: 'More, more, keep going, don't stop.'

We took the Bob Dylan song and made it our own by improvising the melody and changing the lyrics to, 'But it's OK now. Jonathan is safe; we're all safe.' I had no idea where these words had come from but every time I sang them, Jonathan would stare at me with huge wide eyes and raise his hands triumphantly into the path of the Soundbeam, creating his own electrifying response. As the session drew to a close and I moved to the side of his wheelchair, he reached out and placed his hand on my arm. This was very new; there had never been any physical contact between us before and I waited to see if this had been intentional on his part. Jonathan looked straight into my eyes and left his hand exactly where it was. Eventually we said goodbye in our usual way but by now everything had begun to feel different and I was in no hurry to leave.

Joan and I sat in her kitchen drinking tea; she'd been next door, as usual, throughout the session and I wondered if she was going to comment on the music.

'That was quite something, my dear,' she said. I sat quietly, not sure how to respond. 'I couldn't help hearing what you were singing; it sounded important.'

'Well,' I replied, 'it felt important, too. Jonathan seems different, closer, warmer maybe—I'm just not sure. I wanted him to know he was safe and that he'll always be safe, whatever happens. I'm sorry, I'm not explaining it very well but it seemed to come from nowhere…'

She placed her hand on mine. 'You mustn't apologise, dear. Something special is happening.'

'Maybe,' I said, 'but I don't know what it is.'

Joan looked straight at me and said, 'No, but I think *I* do.'

I left the farm that day feeling tired and emotionally drained. I knew that something had changed. Jonathan's behaviour had been so different and it had left me feeling very close to him and yet uncertain and concerned. What had Joan meant when she'd said she thought she understood what might be going on? I hadn't asked. She'd seemed concerned, too, and the mysterious bond between her and Jonathan was a boundary that I wasn't ready to cross.

The following morning I left home just before 8 a.m. and made my way to Bristol University to begin my first day of training as a music therapist. At lunchtime I turned on my mobile phone and picked up a voice message from Joan to tell me that Jonathan had died at home at 8 o'clock that morning. Her voice was calm and peaceful. 'I'm okay,' she said. 'It was very peaceful and he was ready to go.'

I was shocked and upset but stranded in a residential weekend at university that I had to survive and so I kept the news to myself. I spoke to Joan briefly that evening.

'It was lovely,' she said. 'Desperately sad to say goodbye but he was ready. He told me he was ready.'

A few weeks later, at Jonathan's funeral during a private moment with Joan, I remarked on the coincidence of the timing of Jonathan's death and the beginning of my training as a music therapist.

'Oh, my dear,' she said, 'that's not a coincidence. He simply waited until he was sure you were on your way.'

I will always associate Jonathan with my decision to become a music therapist. I don't think that I've ever felt that he's not been around, somewhere, probably giving me a long hard look. There's so much that happened in those few short months that I've never been able to explain, but over the years I've grown very comfortable with simply being a part of the mystery. Joan has her own way of explaining that last remarkable day. 'It was the very best thing you ever did, my dear. The last time you saw Jonny, you let me know that something was very different and so I stayed with him in his room, all night, and I was there with him when he died. That was your gift to both of us.'

As I struggled to come to terms with my grief, I wrote a long letter to Jonathan, remembering our first meeting and subsequent sessions at the farm. In the final paragraph I wrote, 'Well, Jonathan, I don't quite know what to do with all of these feelings but I suppose that one day I'll have to do what I always do, and put them into a song.' I note as I write this today that my song for Jonathan has yet to be written.

RICK

A SONG FOR PADDY: PART ONE

Let the beauty we love be what we do.
There are hundreds of ways to kneel and kiss the ground.
Rumi

'I can't do music. I just can't. Not anymore. Every song I hear makes me think of Jane, my wife, and I just cry like a baby. It's bloody stupid, isn't it, don't you think? With everything that's going on for us, the thing that really scares me is…bloody music. It's crazy!'

We were sitting together in the music room, me with my guitar and Rick hunched over a metallophone, a mallet in each hand, peering reluctantly at the tuned bars, looking frail and vulnerable. In his late 50s, he was a big man with gentle eyes and a kind face; still handsome despite the obvious signs of his illness. I'd only been working at the hospice for a couple of months but I was already learning not to take the power of musical association for granted, particularly here, where the links between memory, music and emotion needed to be treated with respect and sensitivity. It was easy to get it wrong.

I'd recently introduced myself to a new patient, Nena, an elderly lady from Greece, and I'd begun to talk about my love for the Islands and the traditional music I'd encountered there. I'd asked her if she listened to a lot of traditional Greek music, assuming that she must love it. She'd gestured to me to move closer and then quietly told me that she'd been born in a town called Kalavryta where, in December 1943, all the local men and boys, over 400 of them, had been rounded up by the German Army and machine-gunned to death. Together with all the women and surviving small children, she'd been forced to witness this atrocity and had been locked in the town church, which was set ablaze. Someone, an Austrian soldier, she believed, sacrificed his life and managed to open the doors so that they could escape. Later, she and the rest of the survivors had recovered the bodies of their loved ones, including her grandfather, father and brothers, and buried them by the river. Her family had been renowned bouzouki players and their instruments were buried with them.

'Every day,' she'd said to me, 'I dream of a beautiful bird rising from their graves and flying high above the river, carrying their souls. And every day I can tell you that this bird never makes it to the other side. The weight of all the sadness is just too much.'

I'd sat and listened in horror; it was a salutary lesson and one that I wasn't going to forget in a hurry. Music will always have the ability to provoke powerful emotional responses and I needed to tread carefully with Rick.

'It's okay to cry, isn't it, Rick?' I asked. 'It might help.'

'No, I really don't want just to sit here and cry,' he replied. He'd been playing gingerly on the metallophone and had accidentally played the first few notes of 'You Are My Sunshine'. 'No, I can't do this,' he continued. 'We'll just have to try another day.' He placed the beaters on the metallophone and started to stand up.

'It's okay, Rick. We don't have to play music; we can just talk if you like. Tell me something about yourself, something you'd like me to know.'

'Phew,' he said, letting out a long sigh. 'Well, I love music, but you already know that, don't you?' I smiled at him and immediately he began to cry. 'This is bloody hopeless,' he muttered, taking long deep breaths to try to control his emotions. 'You must be wondering what's hit you.'

'Yes, you're not kidding,' I replied, smiling at him. 'People *never* normally cry in here!' We both started to giggle and Rick smiled for the first time since he'd entered the music room. 'Maybe you could make up your own song,' I suggested. 'Something new, you know. Something you've never done before.'

'That sounds a bit…random. How would I do that?'

'Well,' I replied, 'it's not as random as you think. You could, perhaps, write a message to someone, share a secret maybe, or tell someone how much you love them.' Rick was starting to well up again. 'Or tell a story,' I added quickly. 'Yes, tell a story, something you've never told before maybe. And we could turn it into a song; a new song.'

'I don't know, Bob. Still sounds a bit random, if you ask me. You know, my head is full of so much stuff at the moment and…' Rick paused to gather his emotions again. I knew from his referral form that his prognosis was very poor. A few months maybe, at best. '…and I'm struggling to get much sleep, you know, and then when I finally *do* sleep, well, the dreams, I can't tell you…they're so vivid.'

'Do you remember them?' I asked.

'Yes, I do. Didn't used to but now, yes, they really stay with me. It's mostly Mum and Dad. Weird, isn't it? Why would I keep dreaming about Mum and Dad?' He looked at me and I smiled back. 'Okay,' he said, 'maybe that's a stupid question.'

'It's not a stupid question at all,' I replied. 'It's extraordinary how we begin to prepare ourselves. I think our dreams have a job to do; they're telling us something.'

'Hmmm. You might be right. Actually, I've been dreaming a lot about Paddy.'

'Paddy?' I asked.

'Yes, Paddy. He was this man from a rich family out near where we lived. He was really well educated, you know, but there was something about him, something…odd, and his family had thrown him out. At least I think that's what had happened. Anyway, he was left to wander around in the hills near where my family lived, where I grew up. He'd built himself a little shack—we called it his chicken coop—and once a week he'd come down from the hills to collect his money, his inheritance I think it was, and get a few supplies. He'd always have a few beers in town and then call in on my mum who'd give him things, you know, water and stuff. And then he'd wander off and disappear in the hills again. I used to be terrified of him.'

I'd been scribbling down a few notes as he'd told me the story and I showed him the sheet of paper. 'This looks like food for a song to me, Rick.'

'D'you think so? Really?'

'Yes,' I replied and handed him the paper and a pen. I picked up my guitar and asked, 'What kind of song would you like it to be, Rick? What kind of style?'

'Well, I suppose it could be a Simon and Garfunkel song, couldn't it? I love their songs.'

'Okay,' I said and began to fingerpick a few chords on my guitar, simple folk phrases, while Rick looked down at the words and picked up the pen. I sang the first line to him: *An educated man, left to wander in the hills.*

'"All alone",' he added. 'He was all alone.'

'Great,' I said, 'we've got the first line.'

'This is mad. I've never done anything like this.'

'You're doing great,' I replied. 'Keep going.'

Within fifteen minutes, Rick assembled the first verse, adding some new words to create the lyrical shapes to match the music. It was a lovely creative moment to share with him. He'd had absolutely no idea that he could do this kind of thing, let alone be able to accomplish it with such natural and instinctive flair.

'This is a song for Paddy,' he added at the end and I sang the completed verse back to him. His face was a mixture of surprise and delight. 'At least I'm not bloody crying!'

'Okay, second verse then,' I encouraged. 'What happened to Paddy?'

'Well, you'll need to know the whole story.'

During the Second World War, before Rick or Paddy had been born, there was a prisoner of war camp not too far from the family home. By all accounts it had been a pretty peaceable place where the prisoners were allowed to treat the buildings as their temporary homes; in some cases, even building their own chapels and memorial sites. Rick's father had been a builder and had been commissioned to do some work there. He got to know several of the prisoners quite well and, as the result of a compassionate arrangement, he'd been able to strike a deal with one of the POWs. The family would share their Christmas meal with him and, in return, he would do some decorating at their house. Apparently they all got on famously and upon returning to Germany at the end of the war, the young decorator purchased a gift for them, a Hohner harmonica in a presentation box, which he sent to them in England enclosing a note saying, 'Thank you for your humanity.'

The harmonica became a treasured possession within the family, stored carefully in its box in the big 'special' sideboard's top drawer. The years passed. Rick was born and his father occasionally allowed him when he was young to play the harmonica on the strict understanding that he was to take great care of it and cherish it as he would a precious friend. One late spring afternoon, Rick took the harmonica out into the garden and sat beneath one of the apple trees to play. He didn't know how to use the instrument but he liked its noise and the strange writing on its silver case.

He described the idyllic scene to me: a little boy sitting in the sunshine, apple blossom gently falling into his lap. And then, suddenly, a shadow appeared; a rustle in the grass. Rick opened his eyes to find that Paddy, the terrifying man from the hills, was standing right in front of him, swaying. Rick's first thought was to run but he was too frightened to move. He was glued to the spot, absolutely terrified. Paddy moved closer and sat down in the grass next to him under the tree. He pointed to the harmonica, smiled and tried to take it. Rick tried to resist but he was much too scared and, in the end, he simply handed it over.

At this point Rick paused for a moment to look at me and then said, 'The most amazing thing happened. I thought he was just going to steal it but Paddy placed the harmonica into both of his palms, raised it to his lips and began to play it. I mean, *really* play it. Man, he could play!'

'What did he play, Rick?'

'"You Are My Sunshine". He played "You Are My Sunshine". And it was beautiful, really beautiful. I can't explain it but all of a sudden, I felt safe with him. I wasn't scared anymore, not when he could play so beautifully. He looked so gentle when he played, you know; there was a kind of tenderness. He only played for a little while, then he wiped the harmonica on his sleeve and handed it back to me, smiled at me and then he was gone. We didn't speak a word.' Rick paused for a moment, clearly lost in the memory.

'Paddy was my hero really,' he said eventually. 'I'd thought he was a monster at first but actually he was just shy and gentle. I used to go and sit and watch him in the hills sometimes. My kids swear that over the years I've built my own version of a chicken coop in the garden; I suppose they're right really.' Rick chuckled to himself. 'In many ways he shaped my life. I've always been a bit of a loner, like Paddy, I guess.'

'And gentle, and tender, too?' I asked.

'Maybe. Too soft sometimes, that's for sure.'

I'd made a few notes as Rick had recounted the story and he soon began to compile the second verse of the song, playing with the words while I sang them back to him.

'This is amazing,' he exclaimed. 'I can't wait for Jane to hear it.'

As we got close to completing the second verse, there was a knock on the door and a reminder that Rick's transport was waiting to take him home.

'Can I come back?' he asked.

'Of course you can, Rick,' I replied, reaching for my diary.

'I could come back later this week if you have the time; I'd really love to finish this.' Rick was smiling but there was also a sense of urgency in his voice.

'Yes, I'm sure I can sort that out. Thursday afternoon, at two?'

'Perfect, that would be great.'

We walked through the garden together and I watched as the volunteer driver helped him into his car.

'I can't believe I've done this,' he said through the open window.

'It's brilliant, Rick,' I replied. 'Look forward to seeing you on Thursday.'

I walked back to the music room and played the song through a few times, making a rough recording so that I wouldn't forget it. I'd been writing songs all my life but collaborating with clients in this way was very, very new to me. It felt organic and natural but certainly not like anything I'd read in any of my music therapy text books. *Let's see what Thursday brings*, I thought to myself and filed Rick's words away.

When Rick failed to arrive for our next session, I was immediately concerned; he'd been so enthusiastic about coming back and I was convinced that something must be wrong. My fears were confirmed when one of the nurses called me to say that Rick was very ill and was currently in the Emergency Assessment Unit. They were going to let me know how he was doing. When no word had arrived by Friday morning, I called the unit for an update and they told me that Rick had died in the early hours. 'His family were all here with him,' the nurse told me. 'He was peaceful. Sorry.'

I replaced the receiver, feeling numb. I was still very new in post, just a few months, and this was my first experience of a client dying unexpectedly. I knew, of course, that Rick was going to die, but now? Like this? We had unfinished business and his death felt very sudden, brutal almost. The unpredictability of working in palliative care was something with which I would become very familiar. In time I would learn that even the briefest of interventions could make a positive difference but at this moment all I could feel were shock and sadness. I read through the lyric sheets a few times. Rick had seemed such a creative and gentle man and the story of Paddy had touched me. *Perhaps I'll finish the song for Rick one day*, I thought to myself and reluctantly filed his words away.

I was still thinking about Rick, Paddy and the song when the call came from his family a few weeks later. 'Hello, Bob. My name's Alex. You met my dad, Richard, a few weeks ago.' It took me a few moments to make the connection. 'Rick, he was a patient. He started to make up a song.'

'Yes. Hi, Alex. I remember your dad, of course. How are you…and your family?'

'Well, we're sort of okay, thanks. Just trying to get past the funeral, you know. And Mum is finding it pretty hard really.'

'Yes, I'm sure,' I replied. 'I only met your dad once; he was a lovely man. It all seemed to happen very quickly. It must've been very difficult for you all.'

'Well,' he replied, 'we knew that Dad was quite ill but…it was still very sudden, you know. I don't think you can ever prepare for these things, can you? Anyway, the reason I'm calling is that my dad told us about the song and, well, not long before he died, he asked us to finish it for him.'

'Finish the song, you mean?' I was stunned.

'Yes, he'd hardly stopped talking about it and we said yes, of course, we promise to finish it for you. But, I mean, none of us have ever done anything like this so we're wondering if you wouldn't mind helping us. He was proud of what he'd started with you and it would mean a lot, particularly to Mum, if we could finish it. What do you think?'

'Of course, yes, I'd love to help.'

'That's great, thank you. What do we need to do?'

'Do you know, Alex, I'm not really sure,' I replied and we both giggled nervously. 'This is definitely a first for me, too, so perhaps we can just meet and I'll show you the notes that your dad made and we can see where it goes from there. How does that sound?'

'Great. Listen, we can't come to the hospice. Mum's just not ready for that yet so can you come here instead?'

I agreed and we arranged a time to meet at the family home early the following week. After Alex had hung up, I took the lyric sheets out of the filing cabinet again and spread them out in front of me. This had all happened in a matter of minutes and I was delighted to be in touch with Rick's family. But as I sat in the music room thinking about what we'd agreed to do, I began to realise that there were several issues I'd need to consider very carefully indeed. In particular there was the collective grief that I would almost certainly be engaging with to re-open the process of writing the song. Quite clearly this was going to be a song that wasn't for Paddy alone and I wasn't sure that I knew what I was doing.

A SONG FOR PADDY: PART TWO

A few days later, as I drove through the city to the meeting, I thought through the session that I'd recently had with Julia, my clinical supervisor. 'You're doing what?' had been her first response when I'd told her.

'Emmm … I'm going to meet a family who want to finish writing a song that a client had started, just before he died.'

'You're writing a song, with a family, at their home?'

'Yes. Well, actually finishing a song that my client had started to write. But yes, I'm going to their house.'

'Do you know who'll be there?'

'Well, I know that his son Alex will be there, because he's arranged this, and Alex's mum will be there, too, but as for the rest of the family, I don't know.'

'Tell me about the song.'

'It's about an experience he had as a little boy. A strange man who he'd been terrified of suddenly appears by his side and there's a magical moment with a musical instrument that seems to change everything. Rick described it as a formative moment in his young life. We'd only just started writing it really. We had one session and he died before we could meet again.'

'How are you feeling about that?'

'The song?'

'No, how are you feeling about Rick dying?'

I immediately felt uncomfortable, trying hard to keep my emotions in check. I'd been hoping that Julia would reassure me that I was working safely and doing the right thing. I didn't think that falling apart emotionally in front of her was going to help.

'Pretty awful, actually,' I replied. 'It was such a shock; he was a lovely man, and the songwriting thing was happening, for the first time, you know, it had felt so full of…potential, I guess.'

'And so you're grieving for Rick?' She looked at me and smiled.

'I don't know. Am I allowed to? I mean, I was his therapist. Okay, only for a brief moment, but it was my job. Of course he died; he was at the hospice; he was very ill. I've no right to expect anything else.'

'You sound angry, Bob.'

I could feel my resistance rising. Julia was so good at this and I knew that I wasn't going to be able to deflect her question.

'I'm sad,' I replied, shaking my head, 'and okay, maybe I'm a little angry, too. And I feel a bit ashamed about that.'

'Ashamed?'

'Yes, you know, for goodness' sake, I need to be professional. I won't be any good to anyone if I can't cope with things like this, will I?'

'But you are coping. Aren't you?'

'Am I? I feel like I need a good cry.'

'Good,' she said, handing me a box of tissues. 'Try to make sure you do it before you go and see them. I would, if I were you.'

Little by little, I was beginning to realise that, despite many of the lofty clinical aspirations I held for my work, I would need to remember that, first and foremost, I was a human being. It would be impossible not to be deeply affected by working with people at the end of their lives. In time, I would see this as one of the great rewards of the work rather than something simply to be survived. However, as a rookie with less than three months' palliative care experience, I confess that survival was very much on my mind as I took a deep breath and stood at the front door of Rick's family home.

Three young children greeted me. I hadn't rung the doorbell so they must have seen me coming.

'He's here, Daddy,' one of them shouted as they all skipped back down the hall. Alex emerged, shook my hand and led me into the living room. One of the children took my guitar case and Alex began the introductions. It felt like the room was full of people and I did my best not to appear overwhelmed. Rick's wife, Jane, shook my hand and thanked me for coming. Her voice faltered as she spoke and she seemed very close to tears. I was also introduced to Alex's brother, Peter, and his sister, Ruth, and the three children who by now had assembled on the floor in front of the fire with an assortment of instruments including a violin, a recorder and a ukulele.

'Looks like we've got a band,' I said to them and they all giggled and shuffled the instruments around on the carpet.

'Annie's just done grade 3 on the violin, haven't you, Annie?' said Peter. 'Do you want to show Bob how good you are?' Annie looked down at her violin and shook her head, declining the invitation shyly.

'That's great, Annie,' I remarked, feeling her embarrassment. 'Maybe we could hear it later,' and we smiled at each other. The room fell silent and I was aware that everyone was looking in my direction.

'You'll have to tell us what to do, Bob,' said Ruth. 'We don't have the faintest.'

I sat on the sofa and took out the lyric sheets that Rick and I had written just a few weeks earlier. They were covered in Rick's handwriting and I immediately noticed Ruth looking down at the sheets and raising a hand to her lips. With a feeling of slight trepidation, I offered her the sheets of paper.

'These are the words that your dad, Rick...' I said as I turned to Jane, 'and grandad,' in turn addressing the grandchildren, 'had written. It's a story about someone called Paddy. I imagine you probably all know the story.'

'Oh yes,' Ruth replied, 'we all know the story about Paddy, don't we?' Everyone nodded their heads, smiling and mumbling an agreement. 'Everyone around here knew Paddy. They even did a special article about him in the local paper when he died. He was famous, well, infamous, wasn't he?' Again, there was lots of agreement in the room.

And then Jane spoke, very quietly. 'He was tall, well over six feet, and he wore a funny cap and strange ragged clothes. But he was always very clean. People called him "big Paddy, upright and honest". He meant something special to your dad.'

The room fell silent again so I began to read the words out loud, looking around at everyone as I read them, aware that I was bringing a husband, father, and grandfather back into the room. By the time I'd reached the end of the first verse, Jane and Ruth were both crying, sitting together on the sofa, holding hands.

'I'm sorry,' I said. 'We really don't have to...'

'Oh, please don't stop, Bob.' It was Ruth, speaking through her tears. 'We're only crying because it's so lovely. It's a bit like having Dad back for a moment. It's precious, isn't it, Mum?'

Jane nodded and smiled. I looked at Alex and Peter for reassurance and they both nodded, clearly struggling to control their own emotions, as was I. The three grandchildren sat cross-legged on the floor, staring straight up at me.

I'll read this to you, I thought to myself. *Maybe that way I can get through it.*

A prisoner of war, lost and alone in a foreign land
Taken in by family, given a meal and an open hand
Then from Germany a simple gift arriving at the door
Says 'Thanks for your humanity
This harmonica is yours, it's yours'

'That's as far as we got,' I said, when I'd finished reading. 'I know that ...your dad...ended up meeting Paddy one day and that Paddy took the harmonica from him and played it...beautifully. I think that was the next thing we were going to write about. The way that your dad was so frightened of Paddy and how all of that changed. It's quite a story, isn't it?'

'Oh, he loved Paddy,' said Jane. 'We used to tease him about it all the time. In many ways your dad was a very quiet and gentle man, wasn't he?' She looked around the room as the children nodded in agreement. 'But he loved his family and his home and the garden.'

'And his chicken coop,' said Alex, with a grin on his face.

'Oh, yeah.' Jane nodded. 'Your dad and his chicken coop.'

While we'd been talking, Annie had walked over to the sideboard at the end of the room and removed a box, which she now held out in front of me.

'It's the harmonica, Bob,' said Alex. 'We've kept it safe in the family, since 1945. Have a look inside.'

Carefully I took the old faded box from Annie and opened the lid. Inside, wrapped in a dark green cotton cloth, was the Chromonica, an original Hohner 40-reed harmonica looking well used but fully intact.

'Wow,' I said, slowly turning the instrument over in my hands, 'it's beautiful. There's a lot of history here.'

'That's for sure,' Jane replied. 'Five generations of this family have played that harmonica. Oh, and Paddy as well.'

'He's the only one who *could* play it,' said Peter and everyone laughed.

'It was a simple gift, wasn't it?' Jane continued. 'But it shaped your dad's life. When he heard Paddy playing it, it inspired something in him, lit a fire, you know. He never forgot that moment; there was something precious and gentle about it, like him, really.' Jane was crying again and Ruth was holding her hand, fighting back tears of her own.

'You must be wondering what's hit you,' said Peter and I was immediately reminded of Rick's words to me in our one and only session, where he'd made exactly the same remark.

'I'm fine thanks, Peter. I think it's all of *you* I'm worried about. Are you sure you'd like to carry on with this?'

They all murmured positively in response.

Annie, who was still standing in front of me, looked up and asked, 'Will you play it for us?'

I immediately felt very exposed. 'I'm not very good,' I said rather hopelessly.

'That doesn't matter. Anyway, I bet you *are*,' she said, piling on the pressure.

'Okay, but really, I'm not very good. I don't play the harmonica much at all. What shall I play? Something simple please,' I pleaded.

'How about "You Are My Sunshine"?' suggested Jane.

I suppose I should have seen that one coming, I thought to myself as I closed my eyes and hoped for the best.

By the time I left later that evening, we had completed the song. Together, the family had continued to talk about Rick and to share their memories. Annie had insisted that I go with her to the bottom of the garden to see her grandad's shed, his chicken coop as they all called it, and she'd played her violin with me as I sang and played the song while it took shape. There had been some difficult moments in the process and at times I'd wondered if it was all a little too much, but they'd continued to reassure me that this was what they wanted and that it was helping.

At one point Peter had started to cry and told everyone that these were the first tears he'd been able to shed since his father had died. Alex had reminded him how their dad had often said to both of them: 'Be a man but don't get stuck in a world where boys don't cry.' I couldn't help thinking about Rick and how *his* tears had been at the very heart of our decision to start writing the song.

The process of writing 'A Song for Paddy' had begun as a way for Rick hopefully to engage with music in a new way. He'd needed something without an existing direct association and something he could hold onto at a time when he was preparing to say goodbye to everything. He began to tell his part of the story by using the harmonica to link two very different men—a German prisoner of war and an eccentric loner. When Rick knew that he'd run out of time, he did everything he could to encourage his family to finish it. In the end 'A Song for Paddy' became a song about the importance of family, about truth, trust, patience, inspiration and love—and an opportunity for his family to grieve and celebrate together.

A Song for Paddy

An educated man, left to wander in the hills all alone
Lived in a chicken coop, up in the hills which he called his home
And once a month he'd spend his inheritance on beer
Then wander back to the hills alone and disappear
And this is a song for Paddy

A prisoner of war, lost and alone in a foreign land
Taken in by family, given a meal and an open hand
Then from Germany a simple gift arriving at the door
Says 'Thanks for your humanity
This harmonica is yours, it's yours'

And a simple gift can shape a life
A simple act inspire
When Paddy played harmonica to a child
He lit a fire, he lit a fire

From child to a man, stuck in a world where boys don't cry
The harmonica played Paddy's song when the tears stayed dry
His home and his garden became his chicken coop
His wife and his family, his patience and his truth
And the child stayed alive

And a simple gift can shape a life
And a simple act inspire
When Paddy played harmonica to a child
He lit a fire, he lit a fire
And the fire stays alive

A month or two later, I was alone in a side room with Nena, my Greek patient from Kalavryta. We'd had a few sessions together; Nena loved to sing and we'd traded lines from her favourite pop songs, me in English, Nena replying in Greek. But now she was at the end of her life and I'd gone into her room to say goodbye. I strummed a few chords on my guitar and thought about the appalling story that she'd told me on the day that we'd met. And then I thought about Rick and the harmonica; two stories from the Second World War, two very different stories about the same enemy.

I'd planned to sing one of Nena's favourite Cat Stevens songs as a farewell but instead I found myself singing 'A Song for Paddy'. I watched Nena's breathing as I sang, noticing from time to time how her eyelids would flicker, and I knew that she was listening. I allowed myself to wonder what she was making of the song and whether this alternative, more positive, glimpse into human behaviour at an inhuman time could reach out to Nena in the final moments of her life. And in the end, as I said goodbye to her for the last time, I chose to believe that it had.

Things like 'A Song for Paddy' are never simply written for pleasure—they will always have work to do.

ALICE

DEEPEST BLUE: PART ONE

I wish I hadn't cried so much!' said Alice, as she swam about, trying to find her way out. 'I shall be punished for it now, I suppose, by being drowned in my own tears!'
Lewis Carroll

As I sit here in my music room in early June with the afternoon sun streaming through the windows, I'm reminded that it was on a very similar early summer's day that I first met Alice. We'd booked our appointment for 2 o'clock and I was aware that she'd been sitting in the garden by the music therapy room for over an hour, smoking cigarettes and reading a novel. I'd acknowledged her earlier as I'd passed by with my previous client and she'd responded with a glance and just the faintest of smiles.

Alice was dressed in a full-length linen skirt that was much too big for her, which she'd fastened in place with a long lace scarf. She wore a short-sleeved linen blouse and had draped a sweater over her shoulders, tying the sleeves together at the front. Her hair was as white as snow and in the dappled sunlight I found myself squinting to see her face as I stooped to greet her.

'Hello Alice, it's nice to meet you. May I take your bag?'

'You may,' she replied, 'but please be careful. Everything I am and ever have been is in this bag.'

The bag in question was huge and made of what looked like old canvas held together with an assortment of macramé cast-offs. I picked up the bag and Alice gingerly stood up, slipped her arm in mine and we walked slowly to the therapy room. Like the rest of her body, her wrist was so incredibly thin that I made a conscious effort to be very careful for fear of breaking it.

I'd been working in end-of-life care for over ten years by this time and my experience had taught me that these first meetings with clients, even the first twenty or thirty minutes, can have a profound effect upon the potential for a healthy therapeutic alliance and the subsequent relationship that may unfold. Was this in my mind as I carefully ushered Alice into the room and closed the door? I doubt it very much because, in the cool shade of the music room, I found myself simply looking at Alice and wondering who on earth she might be. She looked ragged and ancient, her face and body mauled by cancer, and yet at the same time she was exquisite and beautiful, graceful and serene.

'Welcome,' was all I could think to say.

'Thank you,' she replied and then, 'Before we begin, there's something I want you to know.'

'Yes,' I said, 'of course.'

She fixed her eyes on mine, smiled and said, 'Brahms saved my life.'

'That's wonderful,' I replied. 'How did he do it?'

She leant a little closer to me. 'Have you ever listened to *Ein deutsches Requiem* all the way through, with your eyes closed?'

'No, I haven't.'

Her smile disappeared and she looked at me knowingly. 'Well,' she said, 'you're going to have to, if you want your answer.'

I was smiling now and considering how I might respond to Alice's challenge so early in our first session. 'Would you like to listen with me?' I asked.

'Yes, of course, if you wish,' she said. 'But only if you feel that you'll need some company.'

Alice was in her early 60s and had been diagnosed with breast cancer three years earlier. She'd undergone a full range of treatment, including chemotherapy and radiotherapy, and had been feeling quite well until about six months ago when it was revealed that the cancer had returned, metastasizing in her liver and lungs. Alice was struggling to cope with the abdominal pain and the permanent fatigue; her appetite had disappeared and her current weight was barely tipping at 40 kilogrammes. She'd discussed palliative chemotherapy with her consultant but problems with her low blood count, platelets and BMI had pretty much ruled the treatment out. This much I knew from reading her notes on the morning of our first meeting. The subsequent referral form also told me that Alice lived alone in a bedsit in the city; she'd never been married and appeared to have little or no contact with any family or friends.

'How can I help you, Alice?' I asked.

'You know,' she replied, 'I have absolutely no idea but I think your room is divine. What *do* you do in here all day?'

'That's an excellent question, Alice. Why don't we sit together at the piano and we can talk about it.'

Alice looked a little bemused. 'I'll certainly sit there with you but I've no intention of playing the piano. Oh goodness, no. Music is in my soul, not my fingers.' As she said this she gazed at her hands, turning her wrists up and down and then looked at me with a huge smile. 'These fingers do their work in the sky. That's where they belong.'

I smiled back, tilted my head and said, 'In the sky?'

'Yes. My fingers, well, all of me really, only feels properly alive when I'm flying.'

I didn't ask more about her strange remark. I wasn't sure what to believe as she looked so ragged, dishevelled and poorly. I certainly didn't want to insult her by suggesting that it sounded a little unbelievable that she only felt alive when she was flying, but in truth it did. It was only when I combed through Alice's medical notes after our session had ended that I found a short but significant sentence.

We spent the remaining time talking about music; she asked me to play something on numerous instruments, just wanting to know their names and to hear the sounds they made. Each time I asked her a question or gently probed, Alice would respond with a smile and a long look followed by another question about a different instrument or musical genre. When I talked about what the therapy might entail, she simply smiled and said nothing. Once our time was up, I asked if any of this had been helpful at all and she replied, 'Helpful? This has been amazing!'

I was struggling to see quite how the session had helped. 'Would you like to meet again next week?' I asked.

'Goodness, no, next week isn't good enough at all. Can't I come back tomorrow?'

We made an appointment for the following week and I went straight to her notes and, after a good deal of searching, found the short sentence I'd missed before. *Alice*, it said, *is a pilot instructor.*

If I'd found my first encounter with Alice challenging and surprising, it was to be nothing in comparison to what unfolded over the following eight months or so. She arrived three hours early for our next session and, rather than send her away, the day centre staff had convinced her to stay for lunch and I finally caught up with her as she dozed in the afternoon sunshine. Alice looked pale and tired and as I helped her to her feet, I was again very aware of her almost porcelain-like fragility. As before I carried her precious bag and she took my arm as we walked slowly through the garden to the music room, where she immediately made her way to the piano and sat quietly waiting for me to join her.

'I've brought you something,' she said.

'Really? That's kind,' I replied as she opened her palm to reveal a single white feather which she gently placed on my knee.

'Now,' she said, 'I need you to promise me that you won't think I'm mad.'

I smiled. 'Okay, Alice. I promise I don't think you're mad. Tell me about the feather.'

'Well, last week it felt like you handed me a gift, a key to somewhere new, so this week I've brought one for you. Now, this key has come from an incredible place, an enchanted garden with ever-changing cloudscapes where you can feel all the dust from the stars falling gently. If I'd known you before all of this…,' she raised her arms and held her hands to her face and took a long breath, 'before all of this shit, when I was still allowed to fly, I could have taken you there myself. But I can't and I so want you to know how amazing it is.'

I picked up the feather. 'Thank you, Alice. It does sound amazing. How will I know when I've found the right door?'

'Oh, you just will,' she replied. 'It's blue, the deepest, deepest blue.'

By the end of this session, Alice had revealed not only her passion for flying but also for painting, writing and poetry and I was beginning to assemble the first few fragments of what had clearly been an extraordinary life. I confess that in these early sessions, I struggled to believe fully some of the things that Alice told me. Her creativity was without doubt; she'd begun to bring her paintings and poetry to our sessions and they were beautiful, as were many of the incredible things she would write in the moment with me at the piano.

In our third session, she'd listened to the music I was playing, closed her eyes and asked, 'Where am I? How do I see beauty? Do pictures echo in the dark?' These words became the opening lines of the first song that she composed with me during that session. She described living in Italy, painting in Como, flying aeroplanes all over the world and yet here she was, practically penniless, struggling to get by, living in a tiny bedsit and as far as I could determine, completely alone. Alice was a mystery and I needed to balance the temptation to forensically unpick her incredible story with the overriding need simply to be alongside and support her in what would be the last few months of her life.

Alice soon became a regular visitor to the hospice day centre where the staff were able to help her with some of the challenges she was facing with her diet and the grim aching fatigue that she described as her constant companion. But in truth we also knew that Alice had nowhere else to go; she had restricted access to her bedsit during the day and would often spend hours in the local churchyard, reading books and writing poetry. We agreed to meet twice a week and for our fourth session, I arranged for us to listen to Brahms' *Ein deutsches Requiem* together.

'Make sure you close your eyes,' she said as I took my seat next to her and pressed the play button. The low rumbling opening notes began to fill the room and by the time the first accompanying harmonic instruments had started playing, Alice was crying. She reached over and placed her hand on my arm, where it stayed until the piece had finished. Alice was an enigma; at times she could display an almost breathtaking capacity for survival—her resilience was becoming legendary at the hospice—and yet here, within just eight bars of music, she'd become completely undone. I wondered, of course, what it might be about this particular Requiem that touched her so deeply but Alice wasn't in the mood for talking and we sat quietly for a few minutes until our session had ended. Did this piece of music take Alice back to an event, a trauma perhaps, a person or a great loss?

My research revealed that Brahms had begun composing the requiem in March 1865, just a few weeks after his mother's death. The beautiful fifth movement refers specifically to her as the soprano delivers the tender and impassioned *'You now have sadness, look at me, I will comfort you'*. Alice never talked about her mother and despite my gentle and tentative probing, it was clear that she would do anything to avoid having that conversation with me. She'd described the requiem as the piece of music that had saved her life and perhaps I had to accept that sharing the music with her was the closest I was going to get to understanding why.

DEEPEST BLUE: PART TWO

It was my fifth session with Alice and we were sitting together at the piano reading a poem that she was working on. It had been a stormy day and Alice had spent some time in the churchyard watching the wind swirling through the trees. She'd written:

> *Wildly blowing wind, the leaves must dance*
> *The night of shadows has not yet begun*
> *And we shall dance before the light has gone*

By now we'd begun to talk more openly about dying and Alice was starting to use her poems as a way of expressing and containing some of her emotions and her fears. I was becoming more aware of the sense of loneliness that seemed to sit at the heart of her sorrow and there were moments when I felt I could see its physical presence move across her face. I tried my best to encourage her to bring her secrets into the room but she would become agitated and reach out to her one place of safety—deepest blue.

'Fuck it!' she'd say. 'I need to fly again. So much.'

Alice had also begun to develop her own system of notation, which she would use to accompany her poems to remember her melodies and get me to reproduce them. In the beginning this was easier said than done; the notation took the form of lines and dashes of varying lengths and at different heights on the page. Alice would sit next to me at the piano, waiting while I plodded my way through, note by note, but she absolutely knew what she'd written and would say, 'Yes,' enthusiastically every time I managed to get it right. I got better at interpreting her notation and introduced her to the treble clef so that she could make things a little easier for me, and for the rest of July she never stopped writing music.

The first piece we completed using her notation system was a guitar instrumental which she told me she'd written as a gift for me. It took us two full sessions to interpret and arrange the music to her satisfaction before recording it. When I asked her for the title she said abruptly, 'No, there isn't one. Just call it a guitar piece.'

However, I had a pretty clear idea what was being represented by this haunting melody. On the page of notation, which I still have, she'd written in faint pencil, '*There is now no doorway to the sky.*'

Alice's health continued to deteriorate; she'd tried to pursue the idea of some palliative chemotherapy but her low blood count and ever-diminishing weight had made this impossible. Despite being exhausted she attended her sessions regularly and always had something new to bring. She'd begun to have vivid and disturbing dreams and I encouraged her to write down what she remembered and bring it to our sessions. One day, she looked over at me during a quiet moment and asked, 'Do you know how far it is from the top of the sky to the bottom of the sea?'

I shook my head. 'No, I don't, Alice. Tell me.'

'Well, I don't think I really know myself, Bob, but I'm beginning to see that I've got a long, long way to fall.'

Alice described a frightening dream where she saw herself afloat in the ocean, holding onto a piece of driftwood. She looked to the sky but her beloved stars had disappeared. '*The stars I thought were lit with hope,*' she wrote, '*have emptied out their shine.*' She thought she could hear voices from a lifeboat but they were just the ghosts of all the hope that she'd lost. And when she looked down into the sea, she discovered an ocean bed full of sunken ships, including one that was her own. Her dream poem ends: '*All that was dear to me down below the sea; I cannot hold my piece of wood when life abandons me.*'

'Is this how it feels, Alice? Like you're being abandoned?' Once again I was wondering about her mother, indeed all of her family. Had Alice come to believe that in order to die, she would have to experience the horror of being abandoned again? I knew we were skating perilously close to the heart of her trauma and I think Alice knew it, too.

'Are you scared of dying, Bob?'

'Yes, of course. I believe we're all frightened of dying, in our own way.'

'I imagine you're right. What are people most afraid of, d'you think?'

'Oh, gosh, it's huge, isn't it? It's our final great act, the letting go of everything, and it's something that we have to do alone.'

'But I don't want to be on my own.'

'I think maybe we're talking about different kinds of loneliness, Alice. The journey we take at the end of life, whatever it might be, is something that we all do alone. But that doesn't mean we have to isolate ourselves in order to do it. Lots of us will want someone to be with us, to hold our hand.'

'I'm definitely going to need someone to hold my hand.'

'I understand, Alice.'

'Really, you do?'

'Yes, I do; I'm not going to abandon you, Alice.'

'Thank you.'

We turned our attention back to her song, fully aware that something had shifted and a promise had been made.

Over the following week, Alice became more unwell. She was eventually admitted to the oncology unit, who shared their concerns with me about her lack of support and social isolation. However, she rallied and within a few days she was discharged and returned to her bedsit. We were able to organise some extra support for her at home but we all acknowledged that the arrangements were far from perfect. Alice and I resumed our sessions twice a week and soon she was writing again. One afternoon in late August, I went to collect her from the garden as usual and on our slow walk back to the music room she whispered, 'Here, I've got something for you.'

In her hand was a sheet of paper containing the words and the musical instructions for her final song.

Deepest Blue

Deepest Blue, Midnight Blue
Floating along in the air
Deepest Blue, Midnight Blue
I keep thinking of you

Deepest Blue, Royal Blue
Shadows on land, sea and sky
Deepest Blue, Indigo Blue
Sometime my dreams will come true

Now there is nowhere else to run
I'll be forever with you, My Deepest Blue

Deepest Blue, Cobalt Blue
Moonlight is silver and grey
Deepest Blue, Cobalt Blue
Lights will now guide me to you

Now there is nowhere else to run
I'll be forever with you, My Deepest Blue

My Midnight Blue, My Royal Blue, My Indigo Blue
My Deepest Blue

'Well,' said Alice, 'It sounds like I really mean it this time.'

We'd spent over an hour working through her notes and had just made our first recording of the completed song.

'It's very beautiful, Alice; a gorgeous love song. I'm just wondering who the *you* in the song is; you know, the way that you say, *"I keep thinking of you. I'll be forever with you; lights will now guide me to you"*. Is "Deepest Blue" your love song to flying, or is it something else?'

Alice sat quietly thinking for some time before she answered. '"Deepest Blue" is flying and getting as far away from all of this awful stuff as I possibly can. I want to be close to the people I love and I think "Deepest Blue" is where they are.'

Alice began to cry; the first time I'd seen tears since we listened to the requiem.

'Why don't you tell me what happened to you, Alice?'

'No, I can't. I want to but I'm not going to…I really can't.'

'It sounds like there's a huge risk here, Alice; what is it?'

Alice shook her head slowly. 'You know, I've only known you for a few months but it feels like I've known you forever. And all these songs and poems and music, I mean I never dreamt I'd be doing something like this, especially now. You've taught me to fly, just in a different way. And I'm not going to do anything to spoil this. I want to keep it just like this, if that's okay?'

I could have told Alice that I didn't feel I'd taught her anything and that I'd learnt so much from her. I could also have told her that my shoulders were broad enough to bear the weight of whatever it was that she was protecting me from and that it wouldn't destroy me. But I said nothing.

Alice looked straight into my eyes. 'I'm going to let you know when I get there.'

'I'm sorry, Alice. Get where?'

'I'm going to let you know when I get to Deepest Blue. I'm going to let you know I'm safe.'

'That sounds like you're planning to haunt me, Alice?' We were both smiling now.

'Oh, don't worry,' she said. 'I promise not to frighten you.'

Within a few days, Alice was readmitted to the oncology ward and it was clear that she was in the final stages of her life. The care team discussed the possibilities of her being transferred to the hospice but by now she'd become too ill to move and was in a small private side room on her own. Alice had begun to drift in and out of consciousness. I held her hand and sang a few of her songs, including 'Deepest Blue'. And then, to my complete surprise, the door opened and I was introduced to two members of her family. They were clearly shocked to see Alice so close to death. They asked me who I was and how long I'd known her. I had no idea how they'd been made aware of Alice's condition but they were here now and it was clear that I would need to step aside. I held Alice's hand for one final time, whispered a stumbling goodbye and left.

I knew I couldn't face the 40-mile drive home straight away and so I spent the early evening in the music room re-reading Alice's work and listening to her songs. At around 7 p.m. I received a call from one of the family members to tell me that Alice had died. They told me that they'd both been present and that she'd slipped away peacefully. Alice hadn't died alone but I couldn't help feeling that, in the end, I'd let her down. Before I left for home that evening, I wrote my own farewell to Alice.

Goodbye, Deepest Blue

This is the part that hurts the most
It's less than a year since you came to my room, clutching Brahms and
an old linen bag
'Everything I am and have is here'
Deepest Blue

This is the part that hurts the most
In these short months you've written poetry, painted pictures, written
songs
I have them all here, they're playing now

Deepest Blue

This is the part that hurts the most
I've come to understand something of your life, your father, your
dreams, your life in the sky
Your fragile world, your tender heart
Deepest Blue

This is the part that hurts the most
These last few weeks you've talked of dying, you've dreamt of
shipwrecks on the ocean floor
You've let me know how far you had to fall
From the top of the sky, to the bottom of the sea, to die
Deepest Blue

And this is the part that hurts the most
You asked if I would be with you and I am, but I am not
You asked if I would hold your hand and I did, but I've stopped
I've set out three candles, one for your journey, one for your guide and
one for your peace
I've met your family and I've been released
As if my work is over, and it is
But I don't want to say goodbye like this
Stepping out of your room, taking one last look
Making space for your family, like I should
Saying all the right things
Knowing this is your time, and their time
Not ours, not mine
This is the part that hurts the most
Goodbye, Deepest Blue

Two days after Alice's death, I was asked to help out with a gentleman
on the hospice ward. His wife was being admitted as she was in a lot of

pain and he was finding the situation unbearable. I discovered him in her room, sobbing and pleading for help from the doctors who were doing everything they could to make her comfortable. I managed to lead him down the corridor to the music room, where he sat crying. It was difficult to know what to do to comfort him. I've rarely been with anyone who was so utterly inconsolable.

'It'll be okay, John. I'm sure the doctors will get her comfortable soon.'

'I hope you're right. I just can't bear to see her in so much pain. I knew this was coming but it's the thought of losing her; it's too unbearable.'

'Do you work, John?' I asked, doing what I could to keep him present in the room.

'No, not any more. I had my own business but now I just look after my garden and fly my aeroplane when I can.' He started to cry again. 'Can't we go back and see her, now?'

'It'll just be a few more minutes, John. They'll let us know as soon as they can. So, you're a flyer; were you RAF or…'

'No, no, I learnt to fly about ten years ago. It was my retirement present.'

And before I could talk myself out of it, the question was in the room. 'Who taught you, John?'

'Who taught me?'

'Yes, sorry, who taught you to fly?'

There was a knock at the door; the nurse had arrived to take John back to the ward to be with his wife. He stood up to leave, turned to me and said, 'Her name's Alice Rowe. She's taught lots of us to fly.'

I nodded and smiled. 'Thank you, John.'

Several weeks later John was referred to me by the bereavement team and he became a regular client. The loss of his wife had hit him extremely hard and for several months he struggled to find any sense of shape or meaning. We spent many hours together in the music room as John ruminated and reconstructed some of the many pieces of his life, including the hours he'd spent flying with Alice. I confess that there were times when I wanted to tell John about the Alice that I'd come to know; the fact that she'd occupied the very chair that he was sitting in, the coincidence of our meeting and his role in her promise to let me know she was safe. I didn't, of course. It wouldn't have been ethical or helpful and, anyway, how would you begin to tell a story like that?

OSKAR

SOULS AND SHADOWS: PART ONE

Now I will tell you about my brother… I want to tell you about him. It's almost like a saga, I think, and also a little bit like a ghost story, and yet it's all true.
Astrid Lindgren

Astrid Lindgren published *The Brothers Lionheart* in 1973 when she was 66 years old. At first glance you might think that it's a children's book; after all, Astrid was the author of the Pippi Longstocking books and many other stories for children. *The Brothers Lionheart* is like no other book I've read. It's the story of two brothers, one of whom is very ill, and their quest to find Nangiyala, a land on the other side of the stars where you go after you die. As the saga unfolds and the boys encounter what may or may not lie beyond their mortal lives, Astrid draws us into a world full of remarkable challenges and invites us to stand face to face with the very nature of being human. It's a book about fear and courage and love. I hadn't been aware of the book until Oskar began referring to it in our sessions together. However, by the time he handed me a copy, just a few weeks before he died, its significance had become very clear to both of us. I'd never worked with anyone like Oskar; he was a beautiful lion-hearted young man, braver than anyone I've ever known.

Oskar attended his first music therapy session on a cold wet afternoon in April. He was 33 years old, married with a ten-month-old daughter named Liva. I'd been trying to make an appointment to see him for almost three months without success until his wife, Elena, after much persistent encouragement, had finally convinced him to come to the hospice to meet me. They were both waiting for me in reception and as I greeted them and we shook hands, I was struck by how tall and elegant they both were, and very young.

'You okay?' Elena asked Oskar. She was holding his hand and gently rubbing his shoulder with her other hand.

'Yes, yes, I'm fine,' he replied, despite looking decidedly uncomfortable.

'When shall I come back, Bob?' Elena was buttoning up her coat, getting ready to leave.

I checked my watch. 'An hour or so? Four o'clock? Will that be okay?'

'Yes, perfect,' she replied, then squeezed Oskar's arm and said, 'Enjoy, hon. I'll see you soon.'

Oskar kissed her on the cheek and for a brief moment they caught each other's eyes and smiled.

It had started to pour with rain and, rather than walk through the garden, we would need to take the longer route through the hospice to the music room. It was Oskar's first visit and I knew that being there for the first time could be a pretty daunting experience for most people. I made light conversation as we walked, pointing out one or two of the rooms as we passed them—the visitor's lounge, the garden room—and Oskar politely nodded and said, 'Hmmm, hmmm,' but I knew that he wasn't finding this easy and it was with some relief that we entered the music room and closed the door. We stood facing each other. The disease's impact was already becoming apparent; his face and body looked swollen, probably as the result of the steroids he was taking, and he had to check his balance once or twice as he removed his beanie hat and heavy coat.

'Sit down, anywhere you like.'

Oskar pulled the stool out from beneath the piano, sat down and looked around.

'Wow, you've got a lot of stuff.'

'Yes, I have. It's really good to meet you finally, Oskar.'

'Yeah, you too,' he replied but he wasn't really looking at me at all; he was scanning the room, checking out the instruments. 'This isn't what I'd expected.'

'Really?' I smiled. 'What had you expected?'

'Well, I thought maybe we'd go to a church or something like that and you'd play soothing music on an organ…'

I started to giggle but before I could reply he smiled, raised his arms and carried on.

'Well, I didn't know what to think. Music therapy? Who's ever heard of that?'

We were both laughing and I replied, 'Well, whatever else might happen, I promise that I won't be playing the church organ for you, or at you for that matter.'

'Good,' he replied. 'I'm very relieved to hear that.' His accent was a deep sonorous blend of North American English and Danish.

'How are you?' I asked.

Oskar shuffled on the piano stool for a moment and replied, 'How am I? Well, I have a brain tumour, so I suppose I must be shit!'

'I'm so sorry. How long have you been ill?'

Oskar sat upright and looked at me. 'Do you want to talk about this?'

'Only if you want to,' I replied, 'We don't have to—'

'No, no, it's fine,' he interrupted. 'I'll tell you about it.'

Oskar described how, on a Saturday morning the previous October, he'd been alone in his garden looking after the clematis, his favourite plant. Elena was visiting her family less than a mile away with Liva, who was just a few months old at the time. Oskar didn't remember falling over; in fact, he didn't remember anything at all until about two hours later when he found himself sitting in the kitchen, covered in grass and leaves, with absolutely no idea of how he'd got there or where he'd been. He immediately phoned Elena, who rushed home with Liva and there in the kitchen, amidst all the shock, confusion and fear, began the completely unanticipated journey that would change all of their lives forever.

'I have a thing in my head called a glioblastoma.' He was looking at me quite intensely now. 'Do you know what that is?'

'I know it's a form of brain tumour, Oskar.'

'Inoperable brain tumour,' he corrected me. 'Of course, we didn't know that at first. We just thought I'd had a funny turn, a fit or something. But my doctor seemed pretty alarmed when we told him so I got rushed to the hospital for a scan. That's when they found it.'

Oskar and Elena had been told that the scan had revealed a brain tumour and that a specialist would discuss treatment options with them within 48 hours. They immediately contacted Oskar's father, Johan, who flew over from Denmark to be present at the appointment with them.

'Can you believe it?' he asked. 'Our appointment was in a big open consulting room. We were just behind a tiny screen; there were people everywhere. And I, Elena, my dad and tiny Liva were all sitting there, terrified, waiting to hear how soon they could start my treatment. And then in she comes, the consultant, the big mighty doctor.' Oskar had become angry.

'We don't have to do this, Oskar.'

'Oh yes, we do. You need to know. You need to know this.'

The young doctor had sat down, opened the notes and told them that the scan showed a glioblastoma and that owing to the nature of the tumour and the way it had spread, there were no surgical treatment options available.

'No surgical options!' Oskar looked exasperated. 'No surgical options. So what about other options, other treatments, what is there?' Oskar was back in the consulting room reliving this appalling moment. 'She just looked at us and said there's no active treatment and she would get a specialist nurse to come and talk to us then got up to leave. I mean, Elena was crying; my dad was crying; Liva... We were all crying. I told her to stop. "Wait," I said to her. "Do you mean that I'm going to die?" and she nodded and said, "I'm sorry," and started to leave again. Elena shouted, "Stop," this time. "When, how long?" she asked but the doctor just replied, "We really can't be sure," and left to get the nurse. Liva was screaming; we were all just totally shocked.'

Oskar paused; he hadn't stopped looking at me throughout this entire exchange and our eyes remained fixed in the silence, locked together in a visceral stare full of anger and sadness. I took a few slow deep breaths hoping that Oskar would copy me. He lowered his head into his hands and looked at the floor.

'The nurse was nice, you know, trying to help with Liva, but it was just one great big fucking train wreck. And then, when we were all a bit quieter, the doctor came back; she still had my folder, you know. And she said that they couldn't be sure but it was likely that it would be between six and twelve months. And then she left again.'

We paused for a little longer this time and I checked my feelings of outrage at hearing Oskar describe how he was given a terminal prognosis. In training we would sometimes get medical students to complete a timeline exercise in which they shift their life expectancy, albeit theoretically, to gain some insight into how it might feel to be confronted by their own mortality in this way. It's never easy to tell someone that they're going to die but there are certainly better ways of doing it than this.

'I'm really sorry, Oskar. That sounds like a horrible experience.'

'Yes. It was. But we didn't give up hope at first.'

Oskar and his family, devastated by the diagnosis and shocked by the poor prognosis, immediately sought a second opinion. He was seen privately by a consultant in London at the family's expense. Oskar had a good relationship with the consultant and for a brief time there had been a glimmer of hope. Ultimately it became clear that, other than medication that would hopefully slow the tumour's progress a little, there was nothing that could be done. Everyone had tried to be realistic about this consultation's potential outcome but the final prognosis's weight fell with great force upon the whole family.

'So, it is what it is,' said Oskar. 'I don't want bitterness and I don't want to be angry; there's no one for me to be angry with anymore. I'm trying to change my perspective, my expectations. Why shouldn't my perspective change? You know, if I could allow myself to be terminally ill, if this was a real option for me today, I'd take it right away. But I'm not much good without hope.'

'I'm sure, and I'm sure that's true for all of us, Oskar.'

'Really? You should try telling that to the other therapist.'

'The other therapist? Are you seeing another therapist?'

'No way, no, I just saw him once. He gave me a lecture about what he called "the perils of chasing hope". I was furious. I just got up and left in the end. I mean, we've reached the point where we can't even explain what we feel, never mind what we want. But just a glimmer of hope, right here, right now…are we really not allowed any…?'

His voice trailed off and he left the sentence unfinished. We sat silently for a few moments and then Oskar fixed me with a stare, one that I would become extremely familiar with over the following eight months.

'People without hope don't have anything,' he said. 'Now, can I please play the piano?'

By the end of our first session, I'd learnt that Oskar could play the piano and the guitar and had occasionally worked as a semi-professional musician in Denmark. He'd also written a couple of songs which he'd described as absolute and utter rubbish. But in these last fifteen minutes, I also witnessed how the tumour was beginning to rob him of his dexterity. He'd started to play the piano introduction to The Beatles' 'Let it Be' but soon his left hand began trembling and he had to stop and attempt to regain some control by massaging it with his other hand. He'd begin again, only to be thwarted by the return of the trembling.

'Oh, for God's sake,' he said. 'I can play this! I've played it a hundred times!'

'I'm sure,' I replied. 'Just take a break for a moment; maybe it'll pass.'

But the trembling didn't pass. It had become a feature of Oskar's daily life; whether trying to play the piano or hold a fork, his hand and arm would begin to shake uncontrollably.

'Shall we try a different instrument?' I suggested.

'What, you think I should give up?'

'No, definitely not, of course not.'

'Good, because I won't go down without a fight. You need to know this.'

He smiled at me and I nodded as if to say, 'Don't worry, I think I know it.'

It had stopped raining and we'd run over time; Elena had been waiting for a few minutes in the garden.

'Would you like to come back next week?' I asked.

'Next week? How about tomorrow?'

'Tomorrow might be tricky,' I replied, fumbling around for my diary. 'How about this Friday, 4 o'clock?'

Oskar opened the door to the garden. 'Elena, can you drive me here on Friday for 4 o'clock?'

'Sure, that should be fine.'

Oskar turned and shook my hand. 'Thank you, Bob, for today. It was good. I'll see you on Friday.'

I said goodbye to them both, sat down at the piano and started to play 'Let it Be'. Sitting with Oskar wrestling with the impact of the tumour, watching this young man struggle to engage skills that had once come naturally to him, had left me feeling sad and exhausted. Where did music therapy fit into this story, I wondered, and how might I be of real use to him? Over the following eight months, this would become a recurrent theme, central to our work and the relationship that evolved from it.

SOULS AND SHADOWS: PART TWO

For our next session on the following Friday, I decided to suggest that we explore some new ways of playing instruments, particularly the guitar, where I thought that using open chord tunings could reduce the amount of dexterity needed in his left hand. Oskar tried some of the things I was suggesting but he constantly faced the frustration of not making the instrument sound like the music he was hearing in his head. Very soon I began to realise I was making things worse for him. My plan to help him develop new skills was reinforcing the evidence that his old skills were deserting him.

I stopped and asked, 'What are you thinking, Oskar?'

'What am I thinking? I think I'm now shit on the guitar.' He almost spat these words out and it felt as if I'd made a huge clumsy mistake.

'I'm sorry, Oskar. I just thought it might be—'

He interrupted me. 'No, stop, this isn't your fault. I know what you're trying to do and it's a good idea. But I don't think I can do it. I don't think I have enough time and I think it will drive me crazy, as if I'm not going crazy enough anyway.'

'Tell me how you're going crazy.'

'Well, I just don't sleep anymore; I stay awake, all night, every night. I go downstairs so Elena can try to sleep in between feeding

Liva, you know. But what's weird is I don't want to sleep. I'm not tired. Mostly I just walk around the garden; it could be three or four in the morning. It's crazy.'

'Are you worrying?'

'Maybe, sometimes, but mostly I'm trying to figure things out; my mind is going crazy. Like, for example, the thought of leaving Elena and Liva behind, not to be here with them, this is unbearable. I'm not frightened of dying—yet, anyway. It's just...,' he paused for a few moments. 'It's just, when we die, does everything that we are, everything we've ever been, just disappear? I mean that would be crazy.'

'Do you have a faith?'

'What, like God, you mean? No, no way. Not unless he comes up with a genuine miracle today of course; then I'll believe in him for sure!' There was a wry smile on his face. I knew the question was coming. 'How about you; do you believe in God?' I returned Oskar's smile but said nothing. 'Come on,' he continued. 'You work in this place. What do you believe?'

I thought carefully about my reply. The classic response of asking the client why it might be helpful for them to know this was most definitely not going to work with Oskar. Instead I said, 'I don't think you need to have a specific belief to work in this place but it helps to believe that death isn't wrong, although of course the timing of it can be very cruel. I can't even begin to imagine how hard this is for you, for all of you; but I definitely don't think you're going crazy.'

Oskar sat quietly looking at me, gently nodding his head. 'Okay, so what about after? Are we just dust? Do we go anywhere or do we just disappear?' He was pushing me and as much as I could have simply stopped the conversation, I knew he needed more than that.

'No, I don't think you'll disappear, Oskar, and for sure you'll live on in the hearts and the memories of all of the people in your life, the people who love you. I mean, love doesn't die with us, does it?'

'Mmm, maybe not. But Liva isn't even a year old. Will she remember me? Is that possible?'

We were silent for a few moments before I asked, 'Do you ever write things down? Any of these thoughts? Sometimes it's really helpful to write down what's on your mind, regardless of how crazy you might be thinking you are at the time. I do it a lot. Sometimes my crazy thoughts find their way into my songs.'

'You think I should start doing this? At three in the morning?'

'Yes. I do. I think it will help you. You could bring them into our sessions and we could look at them together. You never know, they might end up as songs as well.'

'That would be good. I'd like that. It sounds like we have a strategy.'

'How about we call it a plan?'

'Okay, if you insist,' and for the first time, I watched Oskar's smile make it all the way up to his eyes.

Oskar arrived for his next session carrying sandwiches and his pill box. He also had a computer bag slung over his shoulder. We'd arranged to meet at 2 o'clock and I hadn't given a thought to his diet and medication regime until now.

'I'm sorry,' he said, 'I have to take my meds at 2 o'clock and I have to eat something at the same time. Look,' and he opened the lid of his pill box to reveal an array of tablets. 'Twenty-two.'

'Twenty-two?'

'Yes, twenty-two. That's how many tablets I have to take every day.'

'That's incredible, Oskar.' I was genuinely shocked.

'Yes, that's for sure. Anyway, I have to eat something while I take them so I'm sorry if this is going to be a bit weird for you.'

'It's okay. Would you prefer if we start a little later and you can take your time?'

'No, it's okay. It takes ages and we've got some work to do. Sorry if it's weird.'

'It's okay, Oskar. I can do weird.'

'Okay then. You want to see something really weird?'

'Um, okay... I think.'

Oskar placed the pill box and a half-opened pack of sandwiches on the piano and stood up. 'Are you ready?' I had no idea what to expect but Oskar was clearly very determined.

'Yeah, okay.'

Without taking his eyes off mine, he lifted his tee shirt and pulled his track suit bottoms to the ground.

'There you go. I'm turning into a wild animal. Now that's weird.'

Oskar's torso, from his ribcage down to his waistline, was covered in stretch marks. Many of them were deep reddish-purple and they stretched right across his swollen body. The same patterns were repeated across his thighs. He took huge amounts of steroids and I knew these could cause thinning of the skin and stretch marks. But on this scale? I was speechless.

'That's OK. You don't have to say anything. I just wanted you to see this.' He was pulling his clothes back together. 'So now when I'm taking all these tablets, you can imagine what might be going through my mind.'

'I had no idea, Oskar.'

'No. There's a lot of stuff they don't tell you. But anyway, now you know. They don't hurt, so what the hell.' And with that he returned to the piano stool, took a few pills, had a bite of his sandwich and opened up his laptop. 'I've got a song. Come and see.'

The first song Oskar brought to our sessions was called 'Every Time I See You'. He'd written most of it a few years ago and had originally thought of it as a silly adolescent love song. However, he'd been revisiting it at home and had decided to bring it to the session as a place to start. I asked him to play the song for me but he shook his head and, from his computer bag, produced a lyric sheet, complete with the chords and some suggestions for how we might present the song. He'd clearly been thinking a lot about this session and had made quite a list of the different things he'd like to include. At the end of the list, he'd added, 'Plus any changes/suggestions you may have (obviously)'.

'I'll show you what I want but you're the guitar player from now on, Bob. We'll work together. Okay with you?'

'Yes, absolutely. Show me how it goes.'

By the end of this session, a brand-new version of 'Every Time I See You' had been written and recorded. What had become obvious to both of us during the process was that the simple lyric had begun to take on a new and significant importance for Oskar and his family. The way that we performed and recorded the song reflects this transition, particularly the refrain which continues to repeat the line, 'Every time I see you, it goes straight to the heart.'

The addition of my voice singing a harmony line was at Oskar's request. I was learning very quickly that he was a serious taskmaster. While he playfully teased me about my piano playing—and suggested that my guitar playing standard was only slightly below his own—he did at least like the sound of my singing voice. I think he knew how important this was going to be as, although our work together had only just begun, his singing voice had already started to desert him.

We continued to meet every Friday, often for as long as two hours when Elena could manage the transport arrangements. Sometimes he would bring songs by other artistes to the sessions and we'd listen together. Oskar loved to analyse the lyrics to these songs; he could spend hours exploring connections, searching for meaning, listening over and over again, trying to make sense of the work. During one session he became quite annoyed with a particular Beatles song and how it had been linked to Catholic culture and lapses in faith. I was tempted to say, 'Well, Oskar, it's just a song,' but I knew that wasn't true for him anymore. He was constantly looking for signposts and some of his favourite songs were taking on a new significance.

He began to approach his songwriting meticulously, making long lists of ideas and thoughts about the process. It was the early summer and he would often stay awake all night, looking out onto his moonlit garden searching for answers or inspiration. He wrote a poem for the first time in his life; a tribute to the busy and determined clematis he'd planted the previous year, respecting its ability to fight and adapt but also reflecting on the way that it can sometimes struggle to survive. The concluding verse of his poem reads:

Some have an easy climb, others have to fight all the way
And a few simply don't make it
However, regardless of their journey
All of them need a helping hand at some point
Even if it is to pull them out of the ground should they die
The thought that the dead ones are pulled out in free and fresh air
Rather than buried
Appeals to me
I do indeed like clematis

'Is it any good?' he asked me in typically direct fashion.

'It's great, Oskar. I'm so pleased that you're writing like this.'

He shrugged his shoulders and said, 'Well, I'm not a poet; but actually, I think I'm quite proud of this.' Oskar was beginning to take his creativity much more seriously and it felt to me as if writing 'Clematis' had given him permission to keep going.

One Friday in July, Oskar arrived early for his session and immediately took out a sheet of paper bearing the title 'Souls & Shadows'. There was no preamble. Oskar was very matter of fact and simply handed me the page and waited for me to read it. He'd split it into two columns: negative and positive. In the negative column, he'd written, 'We can only rely on a genuine miracle as no cure exists or more to the point…science is not ready for us. Our pain, sadness and lack of realistic hope is unbearable.'

Under the positive heading he'd written, 'The perfect song will make Elena believe in all of her qualities and the thought of raising Liva alone. The overall feel to the song must be positive and uplifting. This, added to a beautiful simple melody, would be the perfect song. Because we share souls and shadows, Elena, me and Liva are true soulmates. That will never change.'

I read through 'Souls and Shadows' a couple of times, leant back in my chair and we sat quietly together for a few moments. I'd noticed when Oskar had arrived that he'd seemed less sure on his feet and the impact of the steroids was becoming more apparent; his face was very swollen and his eyes looked sore. Oskar was dying and the reality of the situation began to envelop me in its shroud. *This is a hospice. Of course he's going to die; that's why he's coming to see you...* The words rattled around in my head but they didn't make any difference. I didn't want him to die. Should I tell him? This was a difficult moment for me and I think Oskar knew it. He reached across, smiled and tapped me on the shoulder.

'Come on, Bob. Get your guitar.'

We began to write the song. Oskar told me what he thought I should play and I did my best to interpret his suggestions as accurately as possible. Among my many jotted notes from this session are the quotes that I'd scribbled down as Oskar confronted the reality of his situation, asking some huge questions, trying to say what felt like the unsayable.

Should we accept without condition
Should we accept not knowing why
Too many tears, too many questions
What will give us peace of mind

We are souls and shadows, souls and shadows
You, me and Liva, that will never change
We are souls and shadows, souls and shadows
You, me and Liva will always remain

'Souls and Shadows' was the first song that we'd fully collaborated on and in many ways it marked a considerable turning point for Oskar. In the heartfelt lyrics, we heard him finding his authentic voice, expressing not only his sadness and anger but, perhaps more importantly, his belief that the love between him, Elena and Liva would never die, despite everything. It was also the moment when we began to witness the emergence of Oskar as a composer and songwriter —in many ways the person he'd always wanted to be. As Oskar's voice had deteriorated so much, he felt very strongly that I should take over the recording's vocal duties. I was nervous about trying to represent something so personal to Oskar and he did his best to make it easier for me.

'Sing it,' he said. 'I trust you.'

I found myself moving in and out of Oskar's world, trying hard to be the therapist, not to overinterpret or take ownership of his feelings, while at the same time doing everything I could to manage my own. From now on this would be the model that we would use for almost everything that he created. It was a model borne from necessity and I would need to get better at it. After all, summer was almost over and so, according to the prognosis, was Oskar's timeline.

SOULS AND SHADOWS: PART THREE

A week or so later, I returned from a short break to find an email from Oskar in my in-box. This was new; he'd never written directly to me before. In his mail, he told me that he'd made an important decision during the writing and recording of 'Souls and Shadows'; he wanted to release his own album. We would get five or six songs ready and, with the help of some of his friends in the music industry, release them on a professionally prepared CD. This wasn't to be a commercial enterprise, he wrote, more a statement that said, 'before I died I became a songwriter; something I always dreamt I could be'. His email concluded: 'I think that should keep us busy for a couple of sessions. Just so you know, I've had a couple of minor seizures while you've been away which I could talk about for however long you can bear to listen. But to be honest, I would prefer it if we can focus on the music for the next two sessions. Reason being I have 'done' plenty of seizures but never 'done' a CD! See you Friday.'

Over the next two months, we worked at some speed and, despite the obvious deterioration in his health, Oskar attended every music therapy session that we were able to arrange. The songs he wrote reflected his journey through illness in its many different forms. We talked for many hours about his early experiences, both before and after his diagnosis, and in particular the way he felt that he and his family had been dealt with at the hands of the enormous and, in his eyes, sometimes unfeeling health service. He wrote about this in 'Once in a Lifetime', expressing his anger in the very early days of his illness.

I've been told to die in September sometime
I'd hate to disappoint you, it would feel like a crime
There are no second chances here; you don't get to try again
And even if you did I wonder if the refrain would be the same

I asked him to explain.

'Well, it's September and my time's up. But I don't feel like dying just yet. The thing is, if we all got to do this again, what would you do differently?'

The 'you' he was referring to was the doctor who'd delivered his prognosis almost a year ago.

'Have you learnt anything?' Oskar was asking and 'Can anything here really change?'

As much as I could make a positive argument on behalf of the hospital and the health service, it was clear that Oskar was still struggling to deal with the events of that traumatic day.

'When I'm Gone' was another reworking of one of his older compositions that he'd originally described as rubbish. He took the existing chorus and added new verses which reflected his current experiences and feelings:

There is a time for tears and crying
There is a time for peace and sleep
But when the night is really over
The dreams are yours to keep

In the second verse he wrote:

There is no way I could go back again
Back to that place, that place again

I asked Oskar what or where that place was.

'That place,' he said, 'is the utter hopelessness of fighting an illness that I can't beat.'

For the recording session of 'When I'm Gone', Oskar had strong-armed his brother-in-law and a close friend from Denmark, Simon, to sing the chorus. Oskar loved putting them both on the spot, watching them trying to overcome their horror at being made not only to sing but to have their voices recorded as well. It's certainly one of the happiest memories of our sessions together and it was the first and only time I saw Oskar really laugh.

Before Simon returned to Denmark, he came to see me. He talked about the frustration and lack of self-belief that had been a mark of Oskar's past and how comforting it was that now he seemed so much calmer and more at peace with himself. This took me by surprise. I tried to remember how Oskar had presented when I first met him. He'd been frustrated and angry and quite bitter at times. Now, seven months later, much of the bitterness had subsided; he certainly had a healthier relationship with his anger but was he really at peace? I wasn't sure. There were things he needed to do before he died and he was relying on me to help him. We'd become very close, seeing each other two or sometimes three times a week. He was about to embark on his most important project and we were collaborating at a deeply personal level. I felt incredibly close to him and yet, at the same time, my conversation with Simon had reminded me that in many ways I hardly knew Oskar at all.

The autumn was almost over and Oskar was becoming more ill, more quickly. He was beginning to suffer from serious muscle wasting and had started walking with a stick, something he hated having to do. He'd still attend every music therapy session, often with his pill box and sandwiches, still trying to take his medication despite the appalling effects the steroids were having on his body. But perhaps the most distressing thing of all for Oskar was the deterioration of his speech. It had begun with memory lapses and he'd struggled to find words in English that, in the past, had simply tripped off his tongue. As he spoke now, he flitted unwillingly between English and Danish as the two languages melded into one. We had to work at a pace that Oskar could maintain and I needed to listen intently to what he was saying to try to understand and interpret this new language. His laptop became invaluable—his new voice—but even that became more difficult and frustrating for him as his co-ordination continued to worsen.

We were sitting together in the music room, looking at some new lyrics he'd been writing. It was a song for Liva, a lullaby in which he tells her that he, her dad, had existed and that whatever else happened he would always be holding her hand. Oskar had hummed the melody to me and I'd begun to sing it through. But I knew that this was a song that I couldn't sing on his behalf. It was such a powerful and beautiful message from a father to his daughter and we would have to capture Oskar's voice singing the words to bring it to life.

'You're going to have to sing this yourself, Oskar. You know that.'

'Yes, I suppose.' He let out a long sigh. 'But I'm frightened.'

'What's the fear, Oskar?'

'Well, if this is all she will have of me, I don't want her to hear a brain tumour. I want her to hear her daddy.'

'Okay, Oskar. Let's make she sure does.'

Oskar would often find that his speech was clearer in the mornings and we arranged some early recording sessions to take advantage of this. By joining a couple of performances together, we were able to get a recorded version of the song that he was happy enough with. Being alongside Oskar as he sang his lullaby to Liva was both awe-inspiring and heart-breaking. How deep, I wondered, was this well of courage that he seemed able to draw on? And how much longer could it last?

Liva's Lullaby

When you are in bed, but can't go to sleep
Try closing your eyes and think what to keep
Of all you have seen, we will pick out the best

And find a little thought that will give us some rest

Should bad or evil dreams disturb you in the night
I know it can be tough to keep them out of sight
But I hope that you feel I am holding your hand
Close your precious eyes, sleep as long as you can

But when you wake up and wonder what is true
Lay your hand on your heart, that should give you a clue
Just trust how it feels, though it does seem unreal
Your daddy was here, just ask the seal[1]

'Should I be more afraid of dying, do you think?' Oskar's question came out of the blue after a long period of silence. He'd been talking about his plans for his album, *Souls and Shadows*, and we'd been listening to some of the recordings.

'No, I don't. Do you?'

'No, I don't…but I know that *you* think I'm going somewhere, like heaven or something, don't you?'

I smiled and our eyes met. 'No, well yes. I mean, I don't know about heaven and all that stuff. But, yes, I believe you're going to go somewhere.'

'Oh, come on! You never tell me what you're *really* thinking; don't make me guess. Come on. It'll be our secret, like in *The Brothers Lionheart*.' Oskar was grinning and he wasn't going to let this go.

'*The Brothers Lionheart*?'

'What, you don't know *The Brothers Lionheart*? Like, the greatest book ever written?'

'No, I don't. What is it?'

Oskar was shaking his head in disbelief.

'It's about Scotty and Jonathan; they're brothers. Scotty is seriously ill; he's dying and Jonathan tells him about this place, Nangiyala, where we all go when we die. But Scotty is scared because he doesn't know how to find Nangiyala without Jonathan; he doesn't think he can do it on his own. Jonathan tells Scotty that he'll be there too one day and that he should wait for him; time doesn't mean the same thing there so it won't feel like he has to wait forever.'

'What,' I asked, 'is Nangiyala—is it paradise or something?'

Oskar shook his head. 'Mmm, I don't know about paradise. Nangiyala is a place where amazing things happen, great adventures, all the time. You want to come?'

'It sounds great, Oskar.'

'So, come on, you have to tell me now. What do you think?'

I took a deep breath. Professionally I knew that I could deflect his question but, in that moment, I also knew that I had to tell him. 'OK, the first thing is… You're going to think I'm crazy.'

Oskar smiled and nodded. 'That's okay.'

'And the second thing is… I don't know if I should be telling you at all. I don't know if it's helpful.'

'Come on,' he said. 'I gave you my Nangiyala. Right now, I need you to give me yours.'

I took another long, deep breath. 'When I was a kid, around ten years old, I had an operation on my head. I'd been ill for a while and it was a serious operation. They did it on a Sunday and I can remember bits of the following day, the Monday, mostly because I can remember the pain. I was just a kid but they'd put me on a men's ward and my bed was next to the TV. I remember lying there with my head exploding and the theme music to *Coronation Street* blaring out. When I woke up again, the pain had gone, completely. I felt very weird; it's hard to explain really, just totally different. Every time I closed my eyes, I saw an old man at an old wooden gate and a field full of yellow corn that went on for ever and ever and ever; it just didn't stop. And then I remembered flying around the ceiling. Apparently I even apologised to one of the nurses for flying so close to her head when she was running down the stairs.

'That evening when I lay in bed, the *Coronation Street* theme came on again. I sat up and said to the man in the next bed, "That's not right," because *Coronation Street* was on Mondays and Wednesdays and this was Tuesday. But of course it wasn't; it was Wednesday and somehow I'd managed to lose an entire day. Not only that but I'd also been able to fly, including up and down stairs. I'd been to an amazingly beautiful place, like another world. I'd met a stranger there who'd said, "Come on, Robert. It's time to go," and then somehow I'd managed to return to my hospital bed.' I paused. I'd only told this story to a few people and no matter how much sincerity I tried to inject into it, I could never get it right. *You must think I'm mad*, I thought. But Oskar didn't say a word; he sat quietly, waiting.

'I saw the visions all the time, for years. Nobody told me what had happened and I think I just came to believe I was mad. I'd have these profound hallucinations and the doctors kept testing me for brain damage. I was readmitted for a while. I never told anybody about the near-death experience, the dreams or my night terrors. And then finally, when I was sixteen my mum told me what had really happened. Early that Tuesday morning, the hospital had phoned to tell my parents that I'd suffered a huge post-operative seizure and I'd died. By the time they got to the hospital and came to the ward, I was back. I don't know how long I was gone for; my mum just said it was "a long time".

'For the first time since it had happened, I told her about the cornfield and the old man and how sometimes I couldn't stop myself going back. She told me that for a while the doctors worried that I may have some form of residual brain damage but after five years of testing they'd found nothing. "All we knew," she said, "is that when you came back, you were a very different boy." We were sitting upstairs at the back of a double-decker bus. I can remember it; my mum was crying but I felt amazing. It was like, "Okay, so something really *did* happen to me. Maybe I haven't gone mad after all!" It was as if my mum had given me my life back.' I waited for Oskar to say something but again it was me who broke the silence. 'I guess you think I'm crazy?'

'A little maybe; I mean, if it was so beautiful, why didn't you stay? Why did you come back?

'I'm still trying to figure that one out, Oskar. I've researched hundreds of NDEs...' He looked puzzled. 'Sorry, near-death experiences, and I've met lots of other people who've had experiences pretty much identical to mine. Some people believe they've come back with a very specific purpose. But lots of people are just aware of being part of something incredibly mysterious. I think that's where I am with all of it.'

Oskar leant on his stick and pushed back until he was almost upright. 'So, you're telling me that when you die, you end up at some incredible place and somebody meets you there.'

'Well, yes…at least…that was *my* experience. I'm sorry. I know it's unbelievable.'

'Yes, it is a little unbelievable. But then, when I was a boy I believed in Nangiyala. And I'm not sure if I ever really wanted to stop.' Oskar started to lift himself slowly from his seat and, as I stood to help him, he placed his arm around my shoulder. It was the first time we'd ever made any close physical contact and we stood facing each other for a little while.

'Thank you for telling me this,' he said. 'I'm glad I know your secret.'

'I wasn't sure I should tell you. Are you okay?'

'Oh, I'm really okay, really. Thank you.'

This had been the first time I'd ever told a client anything particularly personal about myself. I'd decided to do so hoping that in some way it would prove helpful for Oskar, but as he left that afternoon I was far from sure that it had been the right thing to do.

---

1. The seal was their pet dog.

SOULS AND SHADOWS: PART FOUR

I'd been due to see Oskar on the following Friday but earlier that week he'd started having seizures at home and Elena had contacted me. The family's fear was that Oskar would become an emergency admission and end up in hospital rather than at the hospice. I often worked closely with the hospital team and tried to reassure Elena that Oskar would get the very highest quality of care should he be admitted into hospital. However, the impact of their early experiences was still taking its toll and they were adamant that they would do anything to keep him at home until he could be admitted into the hospice. After a few anxious days of waiting, Oskar became an in-patient in one of the family rooms and Elena, together with Oskar's father, Johan, became permanent residents. Other family and friends came to stay, including Oskar's mother. There had been minimal contact between them for many years and Oskar had talked about her in our sessions but hadn't wanted to, in his words, 'become forensic about my mum'. After she'd returned to Denmark, I asked how the visit had gone and Oskar, in his inimitable fashion, said, 'Mmm, some old wounds have been soothed a little.'

I saw Oskar every day and we spent as much time as we could in the music room. He was running out of energy and the seizures were more frequent; we did our best to make the most of the moments in between. Oskar had given me a copy of *The Brothers Lionheart* which I'd read and we spent a lot of time talking about the book; not only how it had influenced him as a young boy but also how the message of the book had become so important to him as he faced the certainty of his death.

On one occasion he imagined his soul to be a speck of dust, so small that surely no one would object to its presence, even if it rested on the most beautiful wild rose.

'Imagine,' he said, 'I can be present without ever getting in the way.' In another session he described his spirit as being like a leaf, falling slowly from a tree, kept afloat in the air by everyone's breath. 'Don't stop breathing, Bob,' he said.

During one of these sessions, accompanied by his father, Oskar wrote his final song. It had been a morning of reconciliation, the healing of old wounds, and they sat together at the piano crying and holding hands. By now the tumour had affected Oskar's speech so much that at times it was challenging to understand what he was saying, something he found deeply frustrating. I was able to help translate at times, having spent so much time with Oskar and grown accustomed to some of this new language as it had developed. Despite all the challenges, he was determined to finish his last song and 'Don't Stop Breathing' was written and recorded in one session with Oskar holding his father's hands and the microphone perched between the three of us. The song is about dying and reflects some of the many discussions we'd had about how it might happen, where he might go and what he might leave behind. But most importantly it's a final love letter to Elena and Liva. He uses gorgeous symbols to represent love, and the images he creates could easily have fallen directly from the pages of *The Brothers Lionheart.*

Don't Stop Breathing

I watched you being there, you watched me disappear
Saw you full of fear, I wish I could wipe away that tear

Songs from a Window

As I witnessed the sense of sadness taking over from anger and fear
Only then could we try to accept that the end is near

But then I saw the tiniest leaf
Too small for me, but the perfect size for my soul
Carried around by the breath of loved ones
Carried by the breath of my precious girls

Down in the valley where the grass grows green
Is a place that nobody but me has seen
The walls are deep and dark and wide
I bet it's even better on the other side

I saw this leaf today, didn't quite know what to say
But it made me realise we had found the perfect size

It's up to you to help me through to a place where things are true
To a place where we believe that tiny leaves keep souls alive

I'm here but drifting away, only you can help me stay
Keep me in mind when times are tough, never forget the fun and love

I'll give you strength to carry on, you must believe I'm watching on
We'll be there dancing away in the kitchen like good old days

Once I'm through on my leaf I'll be there whenever you need me
It's up to you to help me through, it's up to you to keep me true

Don't stop breathing, don't stop breathing
Keep the leaf alive and keep belief in life

Down in the valley where the grass grows green
Is a place that nobody but me has seen

The song contains both spoken and sung words and, despite my reticence, it was clear that it would have to be me who delivered it. I placed my guitar in an open tuning, the one I'd encouraged Oskar to use in our early sessions, and began to improvise a melody. Johan held onto Oskar, who nodded his approval from time to time as I arranged and completed his final song. By this time Oskar was exhausted and Johan and I helped him back to his room, where he soon collapsed onto the bed and fell asleep. I returned to the music room and started to collect up the remnants of paper that he'd left behind. There was a sheet that had remained unused on top of the piano throughout the session. I picked it up, unfolded it and read:

To Heaven and Back (Brainstorm)

Tell me which way to go/which way to look when I get there
Bob's near-death experience… I'm glad you made it back.

We were never able to meet together again in the music room. Oskar began to drift in and out of consciousness and it was clear that he was slipping away. Members of his family began to gather, but I could still grab the occasional few minutes with him alone. These brief visits always felt intimate and sometimes I would simply sit quietly at his bedside. We listened to all of his songs together; his album was in production, which clearly meant a huge amount to him. On one occasion after listening to 'Don't Stop Breathing', he beckoned me close and whispered, 'I'll let you know.'

I smiled and nodded. 'Good, let me know when you're there.' I didn't know if we were talking about Nangiyala or some endless yellow cornfield. It didn't seem to matter then and it still doesn't.

Oskar died on 23 December; he was 33 years old. His casket was adorned with the words and music of his songs. At the funeral we sang 'Souls and Shadows' and listened to 'Don't Stop Breathing'. By now many of the congregation were already becoming familiar with his songs.

The Souls and Shadows Foundation began working very shortly after his death. In the years that have followed, it has provided support, training and equipment to hospices throughout Britain and Europe, including Denmark. His songs have been performed in theatres, festivals, clubs, pubs and people's gardens. They'll always have work to do. One of his greatest wishes was to leave something behind for Liva, something that confirmed beyond doubt that she did have a daddy named Oskar and that he'd loved her very much. I met Liva shortly after her fourth birthday and she sat with me in the music room, exactly where her father had sat before her. She was bossy, like her dad, and wanted to have a go on every single instrument. At one point I began to play the introduction to 'Liva's Lullaby' and was told very briskly and in no uncertain terms to 'stop!'

'That's *my* song,' she said, 'mine and *Daddy's*.'

About two months after Oskar had died, I woke up startled in the middle of the night with a new song playing in my head, complete with melody and lyrics. It had appeared from nowhere. It was the day of our annual service of Remembrance at the hospice and when I arrived I decided to change the music programme and sang this new song from memory as if I'd known it forever. I hadn't even written it down. The song was called 'Heaven' and I knew it had come from Oskar.

EILEEN

LA, LA

When you listen generously to people, they can hear
truth in themselves, often for the first time.
Rachel Remen

I'm writing today at what must surely be, at least for most of us, one of
the most extraordinary times in our lives. It's late November 2020 and
the world has been in the grip of the COVID-19 pandemic since the
beginning of the year. We've become familiar with being bombarded
by statistics, the number of infections, the number of deaths, the R rate
and numerous other measurements that form part of every newscast,
every day. The casualty list is appalling, with hardly a corner of society
that hasn't been deeply affected. The message to us all is clear—follow
the science—and so we do. The clinical analysis and the numbers are
gathered together to become the primary drivers behind our decisions.

It's inevitable, I suppose, that in all of this it can be the very
humanness of what we're experiencing that gets left behind. There's a
trade-off to be negotiated—the protection of large groups of people
versus the risk of heartbreak and a lonely death. We witness TV
footage of family members clawing at chain fences to touch, perhaps
for the last time, the person they love. If it's true that how we care for

each other at the very end of our lives is a true reflection of our own humanity, then where do these images leave us, I wonder? We can be empathic but even empathy can become exhausting at times, particularly when we're faced with difficult situations that feel unsolvable. In the end, we look away and stop listening.

Eileen was 90 years old when I met her. She was a resident in a care home that housed 64 elderly people, all of whom were suffering from dementia or Alzheimer's disease. The home was spread over two floors, with the upstairs occupied by the residents who were deemed to be the most ill. I'd been to the care home on a couple of previous occasions to run taster sessions where the staff could get a closer look at music therapy, and me. The sessions had gone well; the residents had responded positively. I was beginning to find my feet in an environment that felt profoundly different from that of the hospice where I was already working.

'I've got an urgent job for you.' It was the manager of the care home who'd met me at the front door and beckoned me into her office.

'Sure,' I replied, 'what can I do?'

'There's a lady upstairs,' she said. 'Eileen. Now, Eileen's been with us for quite a while but we don't know that much about her; she never has visitors. She's in a wheelchair; she's very frail, not eating or drinking much, and we don't think it's going to be that long, you know, for her.'

'You think she's dying?' I asked, betraying my hospice roots—if we can't normalise the words, how can we expect people to normalise the experience?

'Well, yes, yes, we think she's at the end, or very close to it.'

'Would you like me to see her?'

'Yes, we would. But there's a specific job we'd like you to do for us. You see, Eileen is driving everybody upstairs crazy. She sits in her chair with her eyes closed all day saying, "La---la---la---la…" It's endless and it's loud. We've tried sitting her by the window, putting music on in the lounge and in her room, all sorts of things, but none of it works. She just doesn't stop. It's irritating everyone and we wondered if you could, well, help her…to be quiet.'

As I waited for the lift to take me up to the first floor, I pondered the irony of my situation. Eileen was my first individual music therapy referral in dementia care, the classic context where we use music to help people reconnect with memory and find their voices again; often voices that we'd come to believe had been lost forever. And here I was being asked if I could help to shut her up.

Eileen was tiny, wrapped in a thick blanket, her wheelchair parked in a bay window with a view across the garden. But she wasn't looking at the view; her eyes were squeezed tightly shut and her fingers seemed to be holding onto the sides of her chair for dear life. Her skin was almost transparent, pale blue in places, and her few wisps of fine white hair hung delicately over one side of her face.

'La---la---la---la---la---la---la...'

I sat and listened for a few moments. Her voice was breathy, dry and raspy.

'Hello, Eileen.'

'La---la---la---la---la---la---la...' There was a short, sharp intake of breath in between each of the words.

'I'm Bob. It's nice to see you.'

'La---la---la---la---la---la---la...'

There were several other residents in the lounge, most of whom were dozing in chairs. Music played in the background—The Carpenters' 'Top of the World'—and a member of staff joined in singing as she handed some drinks around.

'La---la---la---la---la---la---la...'

The care assistant looked over at us. 'She's always like this; aren't you, Eileen?'

God, I thought to myself, *I hope not because at the moment she's a picture of despair.* I asked: 'Can I take her to her room?'

'La---la---la---la---la---la---la...'

'She's only just come out.'

'La---la---la---la---la---la---la...'

'Yes, sorry, but I'd like to try spending a few minutes alone with Eileen if I can.' The care assistant walked over and began to take the brakes off the wheelchair. 'It's okay,' I said, 'I'll drive.'

I tried to say a few reassuring words to Eileen as we made our way down the long corridor to her room but she remained in the same position in her wheelchair, eyes tightly shut.

'La---la---la---la---la---la---la…'

Her room was nice and bright and there were a couple of cheerful prints on the walls, but nothing that seemed particularly personal. I steered her wheelchair to the side of her bed, opened up the small bag of instruments that I'd brought with me and took out my temple bells.

'Eileen, we're back in your room now. I've got some musical instruments; would you like to hear them?'

'La---la---la---la---la---la---la…'

Ping! The clear, bright tone of the bells filled the room and I gingerly moved them a little closer to Eileen. *Can she hear them, or me*? I wondered.

'La---la---la---la---la---la---la…'

There was no change. I played the bells again and this time moved much closer to Eileen, holding them to both sides of her head, looking for any glimmer of recognition or engagement, but still there was nothing. I placed a small glockenspiel on her knees and played a few notes, this time wondering if Eileen would respond to the touch or the physical vibration but again, nothing changed.

'La---la---la---la---la---la---la…'

I heard a disturbance outside in the corridor; one of the residents had become lost and distressed and was shouting for her mother. Two members of staff were trying to help her. I closed the door.

'La---la---la---la---la---la---la…'

I moved my chair much closer to her. 'Eileen,' I said, and then, doing my best to copy the sound of her voice, 'La, la, la, la, Eileen.'

'La---la---la---la---la---la---la…'

I repeated my response. 'La, la, la, la, Eileen.'

'La--la--la--la--la--la--la…'

Had Eileen suddenly speeded up? I couldn't be sure but, in that moment, I decided to treat it as a positive response. 'La, la, la, la, Eileen. La, la, la.'

'La-la-la-la-la-la-la…'

She was definitely speeding up now, taking less breath between each word and immediately I became worried about making her more anxious. I wanted Eileen to know that she was safe and so, instinctively, as if with a child, I sang, 'La, la, Eileen, la, la, la.'

Everything stopped. I waited, took a breath and was about to sing again when Eileen's eyes sprang wide open. My first thought was *Oh my goodness, she's going to scream.* The look on her face was one of amazement and terror and I was sure that she was about to start crying. I did my best to smile at her. 'Hello, Eileen,' I said but she continued to stare at me as if I'd materialised from another planet. 'Hello, Eileen, la, la, la. Hello, Eileen, la, la, la.' I was singing to her now, softening my gaze, trying very hard not to look frightening. Very slowly I reached to my side, picked up my guitar and began to strum an open chord with the intention of singing her name, but I didn't need to.

'Lala, lala…' Eileen had begun to sing.

At first her voice was hushed and I slowed my playing down to match her pulse.

'Lala, lala.'

There were just two notes which she continued to repeat until I changed the chord and she immediately followed my lead and changed her melody. Little by little her throat cleared and her voice grew in confidence; by the time we'd repeated the pattern three or four times, a distinctive melody had begun to develop and Eileen was experimenting with the sound and shape of her words. *Lala* began to sound like *Eileen*, and then *alive* and even *Allah* and she began to alternate her phrasing and lead me into harmonic changes that I hadn't anticipated.

This had become an extraordinary musical encounter and it took every ounce of my concentration to control my excitement at what was happening in the room. After about fifteen minutes of singing without interruption, Eileen allowed her eyes to close gently and sang a beautiful improvised cadenza which ended with a pause that I took to mean that she'd finished, only to open her eyes immediately and begin again. She continued to stare at me but the look of terror and amazement had been replaced by one of utter determination—she was going to sing her song and nothing would stop her. Occasionally her brow would furrow and she'd lean forward slightly, gazing at me inquisitively as if to ask, '*Do we know each other?*' I'll never be sure what she made of my face gazing back at her, utterly mesmerised.

Eileen had been singing for over 40 minutes and I was already late for my next session. I tried to negotiate an ending in the music but she clearly wanted to carry on so I found myself singing an apology and promising to see her again next week. In those early days, I made a practice of always recording sessions to take to supervision and, as I packed my mini-disc away, I can recall thinking, *Thank goodness I've got a recording because I wouldn't know how to begin to describe this.* I left Eileen's door open and as I walked away, she began to sing again, her voice drifting down the corridor. 'La, la, la, la, laaaah...' I could still hear her as the lift doors closed and I made a hasty exit, making sure to avoid the manager on my way out. Shut her up? I certainly hadn't managed that.

When I arrived at the care home the following week, I made my way straight to the first-floor lounge in search of Eileen but she wasn't there. I walked down to her room and peered through the open door to see that the bed was occupied by someone else, a gentleman. On my way back to the lounge, the manager greeted me. 'Oh, there you are.'

'Yes, hi. I was looking for Eileen.'

'Eileen's...not with us anymore. Come down to the office.' I followed her downstairs and took a seat. I think I knew what was coming but certainly hadn't been prepared for it.

'Has Eileen died?' I asked.

'Yes, she has, last week. But boy did she ever go out with a bang! She la, la'd, and la, la'd and la, la'd for ages; I mean proper singing for ages and ages. She just didn't stop. And then, finally, she fell asleep. We put her into bed that evening and that was it; she never woke up.' The manager could see that I was upset. 'Are you okay? She was very peaceful.'

'I'm okay,' I replied. 'I'm just really sorry that I won't see her again.'

We sat together quietly for a few moments until she said, 'It's strange, isn't it? All that time sitting in her chair saying "la---la---la" when really, she could have been singing.'

'Mmm,' I nodded, but kept my thoughts to myself.

Eileen had refused to be invisible. She was alive and she wanted us to know it until the very last day of her life when she sang herself to sleep and died. The recording of her remarkable voice has been played hundreds of times, all over the world. The message that Eileen left behind for all of us is a powerful one. She had *never* stopped singing. We'd just stopped listening.

The Wanderer's Song (On Hearing Eileen)

Woman, I hear you
Wandering woman, I hear you
I hear your voice, words unclear
Striking true, I hear you
Singing, calling

I see you, before this saddened body came
You, a child, a girl, a woman
Hope fuelled, living a life

I hear you, power filled, ascending firm
Calling from your core, your heart
Forcing the submerged, salty depths
Soaring the dazzling, dizzy pinnacles

Alay, Allah, Eileen, A love, Alive?
A mother chasing her child?
A believer entreating her God?
A woman claiming her own name?
The moon mustering the swaying seas?
A life force rousing the hushed dead?

In your song, in your owned words
You are calling your lost loves
They are coming through the silvery blue
Cool, blue milk haze for you
A wanderer found
Claimed

Catherine Baker

TERESA

YOU CAN CALL ON ME

Suffering is only intolerable when nobody cares.
Dame Cicely Saunders

Those of us who work in hospices soon become very familiar with the concept of a good death. Helping people die well was at the heart of Dame Cicely Saunders's pioneering palliative care work in Britain in the late 1940s. 'You matter,' she said, 'because you are you, and you matter until the end of your life. We will do all we can not only to help you die peacefully, but also to live until you die.' These words had a significant impact on me from the moment I read them on the first day of my clinical placement in an adult hospice. I was waiting to meet the therapist who would be my manager for the next nine months and Dame Cicely's words were in a large frame on the wall in the reception area.

'Live until you die.' Over the years that have followed, I've come to learn that for some people these four simple words could become a pathway to hope at the end of their lives, and that for others they could represent the unnecessary prolonging of pain and suffering. Most of the people I've worked with have come to me when all active treatment has ended. The vein of hope that's helped them to get through tests and treatments and more tests and more treatments and days and weeks and months and often years of uncertainty has just been severed. I sit alongside them and bear witness to the bleeding of hope and their encounter with a new frontier.

Teresa knew all about frontiers. At the age of seven, she witnessed her cousin being killed by a falling tree on her way to their shared confirmation ceremony. A year later, she saw her family home burn to the ground in a fire that took her grandparents' lives. Both her father and her brother had committed suicide while she was still a teenager. For Teresa, a social event, a car journey or sometimes simply leaving her home could become a frontier in itself, often fraught with the risk of tragedy. The impact of these early traumas had deepened over the years and her response to the feelings she continually encountered became more and more extreme. As a result, Teresa experienced long periods of depression; she was often profoundly anxious and had become agoraphobic and isolated.

When Teresa became ill with cancer and was told that her prognosis was very poor, she decided that the best way out was to die as soon as possible, therefore she would kill herself. Perhaps the fact that her father and brother had chosen suicide had given her enough permission to feel that she could follow in their footsteps. Although the full details of her attempted suicide weren't particularly clear, I was aware that she'd tried to throw herself down a steep flight of stairs and that her husband had managed to catch her just in time.

Following a psychiatric evaluation with Teresa, her Macmillan nurse had suggested some creative therapy and she'd seemed willing enough to meet me. Our subsequent meeting at the hospice to arrange our first session had been quite brief. Teresa had appeared very withdrawn and we'd agreed a date without exchanging much in the way of words or eye contact; she was treading very carefully indeed and so was I. She was the first new client I would take on following the recent suicide of a patient with whom I'd worked very closely for six months. Her death had left me feeling shocked and angry with myself for being unable to help her identify enough reasons to stay alive for the last few months of her life. 'Live until you die.' It hadn't worked for Hannah and I was struggling.

Teresa had arrived early for our first session and was waiting for me in reception, choosing not to join the other patients in the day room. I took a few moments to re-familiarise myself with the background information on her referral form:

Teresa is 59, married with two children—a son and a daughter—both of whom are married with children and live overseas. She lives at home with her husband. She was diagnosed with breast cancer two years ago, had mastectomy chemotherapy and radiotherapy...now stopped. Now has metastases in liver and lung and has been given a prognosis of three to six months. She has recently had suicidal ideations and has seen a consultant psychiatrist.

It was the middle of March and Teresa was wrapped up in a heavy coat and a thick scarf that was so big it was difficult to see her face at all. In the music room, she took a seat next to me near the piano and slowly unwound her scarf but although I invited her to remove her coat and gestured to help, Teresa made no attempt to take it off. I offered her some water which she accepted, took a few sips and then rested the plastic cup on her knees, cradling it in both hands. She was trembling.

'I'm sorry, Teresa, are you cold?'

'Yes.'

'Would you like a blanket?'

'Yes.'

I placed a blanket across her shoulders. 'Is that OK? Will you let me know if you're still too cold?'

'Yes.'

The room became very silent. I looked at Teresa but she certainly wasn't making any attempt to look back at me.

'Thank you for coming,' I said. 'It's good to meet you.' More silence, followed by a long sigh. Was this relief or exasperation? I didn't really know anything about Teresa other than her poor prognosis and her suicide attempt but I was already conscious of my sense of being in the presence of someone engulfed in sorrow. 'Would you like to tell me something about yourself?'

'Like what?'

'Well, we could start with how you're feeling.'

'Invisible.'

'Invisible to whom?'

'Everyone, my family, everyone.'

'Well, you certainly seem real enough to me, Teresa. Tell me about your family.'

'Most of them are dead.'

I knew from her notes that both of her children were alive and that they had children of their own, too. It had been her husband who had brought her to the hospice for our meeting.

'What about your children, your husband?'

'Oh, they don't see me.'

'What do you mean?'

'They don't see me; they can't see me. I told you. I'm invisible.'

'Can you tell me why?'

'Because it's best for them.'

'Help me to understand, Teresa. Why is it best for them not to see you?'

'Because it's not safe.'

We paused. I had lots of questions I wanted to ask her immediately but I also knew that if we could move into a creative place, this might begin to feel a little easier. I placed my fingers on the piano's black notes and asked Teresa if she'd like to do the same. Very deliberately she reached out and touched three of the black notes in the upper register.

'Just play anything you like,' I said as I started to play some simple open chords. Her fingers moved but they made no sound. I stopped playing and she continued to press the black keys, starting with F#, one after another. She pressed the keys so gently that the hammers hardly touched the strings and the only sound we could hear was the creaking of the piano action.

'I told you I was invisible.'

'Oh, perhaps you're just being very gentle. Why don't you press harder?'

Teresa repeated the same pattern a few times until we w
about able to hear the notes.

'Keep playing,' I said and started to play the same four notes in
lower register to encourage her to keep going. We played this simple
pattern for several minutes without speaking until Teresa suddenly
said, '"Frère Jacques".'

'Yes, it's the first four notes, for sure,' I said. 'I imagine you know
the song well?'

'I do.'

And so I began to sing, 'Frère Jacques, Frère Jacques.'

Almost immediately I became aware that Teresa had started to cry.
Her shoulders were trembling as she tried to hold onto her tears while,
at the same time, she continued to play the piano, as if the notes
themselves were the very things that were keeping her from falling
apart. When she finally stopped playing, she turned towards me and
our eyes met properly for the first time.

'Maud,' she said and began to weep.

Teresa had grown up in a small town in the Alsace region of France
and Maud was her cousin and her best friend. They'd done everything
together. They were the same age, attended the same school and church
and were, in Teresa's words, 'joined at the hip'. Teresa vividly
remembered the day that was to be their shared confirmation service;
she and her father had arrived early and were taking shelter from a
violent storm in the church. As she stood at the entrance, eagerly
waiting to greet Maud, a powerful gust of wind tore up a tree which
landed directly on top of the approaching car, killing Maud and Maud's
parents.

I sat quietly listening to her story. I was shocked, of course, trying
to imagine witnessing such a violent event at the age of seven. I was
also aware that this had happened over 50 years ago when our
understanding of trauma and how to help people survive it was vastly
different and in many ways incredibly unhelpful. Serious trauma can
profoundly affect our sense of reality and, particularly with someone so
young, can have a massive impact on how we develop an
understanding of ourselves and how we might even begin to fit into the

rest of the world. I was confident that in this brief musical exchange, Teresa was encountering an imprint from the past and, as I wondered how to introduce this thought, Teresa did it for me.

'I suppose it was hearing you sing "Frère Jacques"; it's a song we sang together.' Teresa had stopped crying and was leaning back in her chair, clearly processing some thoughts. I sat and waited.

'You like Vincent?' She was staring at the painting on the wall above the piano, a print of Van Gogh's *Church at Auvers*.

'Yes, I do,' I replied, 'obsessively at times. And you?'

'Yes, I like his paintings. But such a tragic life, such a sad story.'

'And yours, Teresa? Your story?'

She nodded. 'Mmm, Maud was like my sister; she should never have died. A falling tree, good God, imagine, a falling tree, how can that happen?'

'It's shocking, Teresa. I wonder how you've survived such an awful experience, because you clearly have—survived, I mean?'

'You think so? Maybe I died with Maud.'

'No, Teresa, you're definitely here; this is real.'

'Mmm, maybe.'

Suddenly I became very aware of the fragility of our developing relationship. Teresa was almost certainly going to die within the next few months and my training, the way that I worked, my whole approach was focused on the quality of the life that remained. 'Live until you die.' And yet Teresa seemed to believe that she'd died a long time ago, or at least a part of her had. I had to remind myself that she'd attempted to kill herself just a few weeks ago and, rather than inviting her to revisit the entire content of her trauma, it would be much more important to help her to tolerate being in the here and now. But there was more to come.

'Shall I tell you about the fire?'

'The fire?'

'Yes, it was a year, maybe two, after Maud. We were coming home from school and we saw the smoke. It was our house; it burnt to the ground. My grandparents were inside. We moved away, never went back. It killed my father; he never got over it, always blamed himself.

It wasn't his fault, of course, but no one could tell him. He stopped listening. He committed suicide, you know.'

'How old were you, Teresa?'

'I don't know. Fifteen maybe. I was still at school when it happened. I can remember that much.'

'Who was supporting you through all of this? Where were the rest of your family?'

'Well, I had my mum but it was all just too much, too unbelievable; we never talked about it really. And then my brother died.'

Teresa began crying again, silent tears this time, lots of them, rolling down her face and into the tissue she held under her chin. I sat and waited, counting my breath, considering how I might respond. *How does anyone cope with such a series of overwhelming events*, I wondered, *and what will be helpful now*? We'd been revisiting Teresa's past traumas at an extraordinary speed and I needed to help her find a place of safety, in the music perhaps, where her responses could begin to return to neutral. I began to play the black notes of the piano again and soon Teresa joined in, playing the same short melody that had evoked such an emotional response less than fifteen minutes earlier. We played together. It felt fragile, cautious and careful but slowly the melody began to develop to the point where I could play some supportive chords while Teresa continued to play the tune.

'You told me earlier that it was best for your children and your husband if you were invisible,' I said. She glanced towards me and then looked away.

'I'm a very dangerous person. You can see that, can't you?'

'I can see that some tragic things have happened to some of the people you've loved, for sure. But you're not responsible for these tragedies. They didn't happen because of you.'

'No, maybe, but I make the world so unsafe for my children. I'm always scared that something awful will happen to them. I hide from them. I don't want to know what they're doing. I'm terrified for them.'

'I imagine they know this about you?'

'Yes, they do. And then it's cancer, treatment and all the worry I've brought down upon them and now, look, I'm going to die. I'm not even 60 years old; so much more pain and suffering for them.'

'What about *your* pain and suffering? Do you really want to be alone and just simply disappear?' Teresa didn't answer. 'You know, Teresa, I think you should talk to your family; you could tell them how you feel, today, now. It's okay. I believe they'll want to hear it.'

We hadn't stopped playing the piano through this exchange. I invited her to close her eyes and imagine that her family, past and present, were all assembled in a place that would have some significance to her. Teresa sat quietly, thinking. I wasn't sure how she was going to respond to my suggestion, if indeed at all.

And then, 'I'm in the field by our old house in France.'

'Good, what can you see?'

'Our house, after the fire.'

I paused, allowing the image to settle in the room. 'Who else is there?'

'All of them; they're all here.'

'Can they see you?'

'I'm invisible.'

'But you're not invisible really, are you, Teresa? Let them see you.' I continued playing our simple melody and waited. I didn't know how much Teresa had committed to this process and had no idea where it might take her.

'I'm watching you from this field of grass,' she said, followed by a long sigh. 'You can see me but you don't need me.'

I resisted the temptation to congratulate her for becoming visible and also to challenge the thought that her family didn't need her. Instead I kept playing, matching the music's pulse as much as I could to her breathing.

'I can see you talking but only hear myself. If you noticed me, you'd run away.'

And there, in just a few sentences, was Teresa's description of the reality she'd come to know, unable to engage fully with her family, her head often full of negative voices fuelling the fear and shame that she'd carried for most of her life. I wanted to remind Teresa that despite the appalling nature of her experiences, she'd conjured up enough resources to survive. I also knew that we would need to find a new way for her to articulate her responses for this to be helpful at all.

'Let's sing these words.'

'What?'

'We can sing your words; they'll fit with the melody we've been playing.'

'I'm not a singer,' she said. Had I detected the very slightest edge of a smile?

'No, but perhaps today you are. Sing with me, Teresa.' And so we began, very tentatively at first, Teresa shrugging and adjusting the collar of her coat as she wrestled with the awkwardness of opening up in a new way.

'I'm too hot.'

I helped her remove the blanket and then her overcoat and for the first time I was able to witness some of the ravages of her cancer; Teresa was tiny. I hadn't been sure whether her refusal to remove her coat had been an expression of her reluctance to be with me, but now it was off it certainly felt more comfortable. She was going to stay. We started again and Teresa slowly began to join in and gain a little confidence. We now had a complete first verse consisting of the exact words she'd used to describe her experience so far, and Teresa was singing them.

> *I am watching you from this field of grass*
> *You can see me but you don't need me*
> *I can see you talking but only hear myself*
> *If you noticed me you'd run away*

'How are you feeling, Teresa?'

'Very weird.' I smiled reassuringly and she nodded. 'I love my family, you know.'

'I'm sure. Keep talking to them. What else do you want to tell them?'

Teresa closed her eyes again and began singing.

Yet I love you all and I watch you all
I am always here, guarding you

From a burning house or a falling tree
You can call on me, you can call on me

The words themselves were powerful but as they emerged, held in the fragility of Teresa's voice, I felt a physical sense of release; was this the shift from Teresa's explicit memories into a new, implicit, emotional response, I wondered?

'I don't know where that came from,' she said. She was crying and smiling at the same time. 'Guarding! What a word. I'd never thought that that's what I was doing. Have I been guarding them?'

'I suspect you have but I guess you've always felt you needed to.' Teresa didn't reply and we sat quietly for a few moments. I looked over at the clock on the wall and realised that we'd been together for less than 40 minutes.

'Would you like to record your song?' I asked politely but I knew that I would struggle to take 'no' for an answer. It felt essential to capture a performance of her song at this moment in the process. I wanted her to know that it was all definitely real. To my great relief, Teresa nodded in agreement and the actual recording took no more than five minutes to complete. I played the simple piano part and Teresa sang her words faultlessly until the very end where she repeated the last line and her emotions broke through to create a final, trembling 'You can call on me'.

Afterwards Teresa seemed very calm and sat quietly waiting while I prepared a CD of her recording together with the page that contained her words. At the top she'd written the title, 'You Can Call on Me' and I inscribed this title onto the CD. By the time I'd finished, Teresa had replaced her coat and scarf and was standing at the door ready to leave.

'Thank you, Teresa.'

'Thank you,' she replied and before I had time to say anything else, she'd gone. I drove home that night thinking about her, trying to imagine her children, wondering what she might do with the CD.

Should I have cautioned her about sharing it with her family; should I have done more to convince myself that she was safe? What, I wondered, would she do next?

It was about a week later when Teresa appeared at my door and I enthusiastically invited her in.

'No, I'm not coming in. I came by to give you this.' She handed me a painting, a copy of Vincent's *Cherry Orchard*, and said, 'I painted this many years ago and I'd like you to have it.'

'That's very lovely, Teresa. Are you sure you won't come in just for a moment? We haven't arranged our next session.'

'No,' she said. 'Thank you but our work together is done.' I was a little shocked but Teresa seemed comfortable and she was smiling at me. 'I've decided to stay alive now, you know, until I die. I wanted to say thank you for your help and also to say goodbye.'

I wanted to ask all sorts of questions but at that moment I was pretty much lost for words. 'Goodbye, Teresa. Thank you.' We shook hands and she was gone.

I never saw Teresa again. She continued to be supported by our Macmillan nurse team and eventually died at home in early September; she'd lived for over six months since that cold day in March when we'd worked together. On the day of her funeral, I lit a candle and listened to our recording of her song. It had been an extraordinary encounter and it was quite an experience to sit in the music therapy room and hear her voice again. As I prepared to leave for home that evening, I noticed a gathering of people in the garden in front of my room. I opened my door to say hello and one of the group approached me.

'Hi, are you Bob, the music therapist?'

'Yes, I am.' We shook hands.

'Do you have a minute?'

'Yes, of course, come on in.' I led him into the room and he took a seat by the window.

'How can I help?'

'I'm Danny, Teresa's husband. You met Teresa here a few months ago?'

'Yes, of course. I remember Teresa. I was aware that today was the day of her funeral; I listened to her song earlier.'

Danny looked confused. 'Her song?'

I immediately realised my mistake and did my best to cover it up. 'No, sorry, it's okay. How are you? How was the funeral?'

'It was a lovely service, thanks. A few of us have come over to say thanks to the Mac team and to leave a donation that we've collected in Teresa's name.'

'That's really kind, thank you.'

Danny crossed his legs and leant forward in the chair. 'I was going to write to you so I'm pleased I've managed to meet you in person. I know you met Teresa back in the spring. She didn't say a great deal about it but I wanted to let you know that something wonderful happened. As you may know, Teresa had some awful things happen in her early life and in many ways, they haunted her. She found travelling incredibly difficult; she was terrified at the thought of the children travelling anywhere. In the end we just kept things from her all the time, to protect her, you know?'

I nodded. 'Yes, I think I understand.'

'Well, she found out that our son who lives in South Africa was going to come home to be with her. Normally this would have been a catastrophe in the making for Teresa. She would have been convinced that his plane would crash or that there would be an accident on the way to the airport; one way or another it was highly likely that there would be some kind of disaster. She would have become very ill in the past, inconsolable; that's why we always kept these things secret. But on the day he was due to arrive, she got up early, showered, woke me up and said, "Come on. I'm ready." I was shocked. I could hardly believe it but she meant it; she was deadly serious. And so we travelled, by car, all the way to Gatwick airport together and when my son and his family walked through the gate, Teresa and I were there, holding hands, waiting to greet them. I know it sounds crazy but I just can't tell you how much that meant to us, to all of us, for her to be there, smiling. It was just a fantastic day.' Danny was fighting back his tears and I was struggling, too.

'Thank you for telling me this; it's great to hear.'

'We just wanted you to know. Teresa died at home; we were all with her…and we had some lovely times together before she went. She was peaceful, finally, thank God.'

'Thank you so much for letting me know. I only knew Teresa briefly but she was a remarkable person.'

'She was that, for sure.' Danny looked around the room and spotted *The Church at Auvers*. 'Is that Van Gogh?' he asked.

'Yes, it is.'

'She loved Van Gogh, you know; she was kind of obsessed with him really. I used to worry about it; he had such a tragic life but Teresa adored him. Kindred spirits, I guess.'

I nodded; we shook hands and said goodbye. I sat for a while, taking in what I'd heard. At the end of her life, Teresa had found a way to transform the impact of her experiences and tolerate the present enough to live until she died. I'd spent less than one hour with Teresa and in many ways I hardly knew her at all but I'd been lucky enough to stand at that frontier with her where, despite all the suffering, she'd found the courage to stay alive.

And what about her song? I suppose that I'd imagined Teresa sitting with her family and playing the recording to them all and had been quite concerned about that very scenario. But I needn't have worried; it was clear that Teresa hadn't shared it. Perhaps there was no need for her to do so; it had been in the creative process itself in which the catharsis had taken place and I'd certainly felt an energy shift when we sat and listened to the recording of her voice singing, 'I am always here, guarding you'.

I looked over to Teresa's painting of the *Cherry Orchard*, which I'd placed on top of my piano, and then across the room to the print of Vincent's *The Church at Auvers* and allowed myself simply to wonder about the connectedness of things.

Several months later I made a short pilgrimage to Auvers-sur-Oise where Van Gogh had spent the last few months of his life. Ever since I was a teenager, I've been obsessed with the story of Vincent's life, his relationship with his brother and his struggle to be accepted. I was feeling a little burnt out and had always promised myself that one day I'd go and put a flower on his grave and that of his brother, Theo, who's buried next to him. When Teresa had handed me her painting of the *Cherry Orchard*, I knew that it was time I took the trip.

On the way to the cemetery on the outskirts of the town, I paused to take a long look at the church. It was a bitterly cold day and I thought of Teresa back in March, wrapped in her scarf and overcoat, telling me that she was invisible and yet here she was today, so present in my thoughts that I couldn't help but see her everywhere I looked.

'Live until you die,' Dame Cicely had said and, despite it all, Teresa had done just that. I may never fully understand everything that happened in our brief encounter on that cold March day but walking in Auvers-sur-Oise with Teresa's song playing in my head was a powerful reminder that the most mysterious things in this world can often become the most beautiful.

NICKY

CHEMOTHERAPY

My heart contains a cavity, once dry and empty
Over the years through sharp, repeated incidents of life
The pain seeped in, then swelled to form a dark, rich lake
So often now my tears spill over
You cannot mend that hole nor dry past tears
But take my hand around the lake we will plant flowers
To make a beautiful display

Jack Latimer

I'd been working with Nicky for about three months; she'd developed graft versus host disease (GVHD) following a stem cell transplant and had been struggling to cope with the physical changes to her skin and the overwhelming exhaustion that often accompanies the condition. Nicky was an elegant woman in her late 50s, bright, articulate and often quite challenging in our sessions. On this particular afternoon, she'd told me that she'd almost cancelled our appointment; she was feeling particularly unwell and was dreading her next round of chemotherapy treatment which was due to start on the following

Monday. Nicky hated chemotherapy. It had always made her feel incredibly ill and at this late stage in her illness, she questioned the wisdom of going through any more treatment, particularly when she took so long to recover from all of the side-effects.

'I'm only doing it for the family,' she told me. 'If it was down to me, I'd stop.' I reminded her that she did have a choice, to which she responded angrily, 'No, I don't! I might be dying when I'm at the hospice but not when I'm at home. When I'm at home, we only talk about getting better, even though we all know it's not going to happen. They just want me to keep on fighting and I don't think I can anymore.'

'You need to tell them,' I said, to which she scoffed and replied, 'Oh really! How do you propose I do that?'

Nicky had started to write a song in our sessions and I'd introduced her to acrostics, a way of creating poems by selecting a significant word and using the letters to spell out new words or phrases. I suggested we try the same approach using the word *chemotherapy* and, after a little negotiating, she agreed to try it.

Nicky completed the acrostic in less than a minute and was genuinely surprised by what she'd written.

Chemotherapy

Come in next Monday to start your treatment
Hold on a minute—I need time to think
Everyone says just do as they say, but
Monday's too soon
Oh!
There must be another way
Help me someone, please
Except there is no one
Ready or not it must go
Ahead
Poisoning begins on Monday
You've no other choice

We started to improvise with a view to writing another song but it was clear that Nicky wanted to have an urgent conversation with her family and that the acrostic, as it stood, could help to create the opportunity that she needed. Later that evening, having shared the acrostic with her family, Nicky decided to put all active treatments on hold. 'I read them the poem,' she said, 'and then we all had a really good cry together. I didn't have to say anything else; we all knew it was the right thing to do.'

The decision had a positive impact on Nicky almost immediately. She was able to relax and to begin creating her legacy in her own unique way. She would often use acrostics to explore her memories and feelings and some of these poems would eventually become songs. One such acrostic led her to write about the tiny village that her ancestral family were from and, before she died, she was able to make the pilgrimage back there. It had a huge impact on her. '*Arriving back home*,' she wrote, '*where everything is warm, home is where I want to be, this refuge in my mind.*'

Nicky prepared for her death with a courage that was, at times, quite breathtaking. She had the wonderful gift of being able to talk very frankly and honestly about dying and then, without as much as a by your leave, deliver a reflective sentence or two that would stay on your mind for days. Once, in the middle of a conversation about her funeral arrangements, she paused to look out of the window at the hospice garden and said, 'Oh, how lucky we are; we've got the sun and the rain. I wish everyone could see that.' By the end of our session, Nicky had written what was to be her final song; it was to be for her funeral and I'd agreed that I would sing it.

How Lucky We Are

Oh, how lucky we are, Oh, how lucky we are
Oh, how lucky we are, we've got the sun and the rain, we've got the
sun and the rain
I wish that everybody could see that
And not drive themselves to death, for bigger cars and better things

Oh, how lucky we are, Oh, how lucky we are
Oh, how lucky we are, we've got the sun and the rain, we've got the
sun and the rain
If only we appreciated each other instead of wanting to change
everyone
We should see people as they are
If you're defined by your achievements what do you do?
What do you do?

A few months after Nicky died, I received a letter from her husband, Jonny, in which he enclosed some photographs of her. '*I just wanted you to know how beautiful she was,*' he wrote. In the envelope I also found an acrostic he'd written using the word Respect.

Respect

Remembering Nicky is something that I do all day
Every day
She is always with me
Probably I think of her more now than I
Ever did
Can I ever come to
Terms with being without her?

I knew from my work with Nicky that Jonny was an intensely private man and I assumed that, in his way, he was reaching out for help, so I contacted him. Over the following year, Jonny and I met every few weeks and, little by little, he was able to come to terms not only with losing Nicky but also the often very cruel nature of the condition that had led to her death.

Neither Nicky nor Jonny would ever have described themselves as particularly creative; I know this from the many conversations I had with both of them. How perfect then, that at a time when they were struggling to find a way to ask for help, they both eventually found their authentic voices in lyrical poetry. We may not have always created melodies to accompany their words but they sang out to us just the same, and we heard them.

DIANA

GRACE: PART ONE

Death changes nothing but the masks that cover our faces.
The woodsman shall still be a woodsman,
The ploughman, a ploughman,
And she who sang her song to the wind shall sing it also to the
moving spheres.
Kahlil Gibran

When I was applying to train as a music therapist, it became apparent that my lack of formal music training could become a serious problem. I'd learnt to read music as an eight-year-old chorister and could still just about manage to read a top line, but the rest was, quite frankly, mysterious. I'd been playing and writing music for many years, learning everything by ear and relying heavily on my improvisation skills. I could read chord charts and a bit of tablature but that was about the extent of my formal skills. It was therefore with a degree of horror that I gazed down at the manuscript that I'd just been handed at my university interview and been asked to play. I'd been doing some last-minute practice and reading in preparation for the day but this was Brahms, in C$^\#$ minor, and I didn't have a chance. I sat nervously staring at the music, waiting for the inevitable.

'Perhaps you can tell us what key it's in?' The director of music was already becoming a little perplexed.

'Yes,' I said, 'er...C-sharp, I think.'

'Major?' he asked rather sarcastically, 'or...minor...d'you think?'

I ploughed my way into the process, hoping that at any moment I'd recognise the melody and would be able to start improvising, but I hadn't got very far before he decided to put an end to my misery.

'You're not very good at this, are you?'

'No,' I replied, 'I'm not. I haven't read music for a long, long time, I'm afraid.'

One of the other professors joined in. 'So, are you saying you can't play this piece at all?'

'Er...well...yes...well...no, I can...but it's going to take me a while to...um... but once I know the melody I *will* able to play it.' They sat silently, staring at me. *Oh God*, I thought, *this is dreadful. I need to do something, anything.*

'And,' I said, 'I'll be able to remember it and play it on my guitar...pretty much straight away...and... in any key.'

'Really?' asked the director of music sceptically. 'Well, shall we try *that* then?' He marched over to the piano and sat next to me on the stool, guiding me through the bars until I could play the top line melody. I picked up my guitar and played the piece in various keys while offering a few suggestions on how we might think about changing some of the harmonies to suggest different flavours and emotions. I could do this because it was the way that I, like most of my colleagues, had been playing music for decades. It had become second nature to work like this and I was pulling out all the stops to convince the panel to take me on. They were kind and tolerant.

I could see that I'd presented them with something of a dilemma and as I left the room, I turned to them and said rather pleadingly, 'Thank you. I really want to do this.'

After what seemed an endless wait, I was called back into the room and told that the panel had decided to take a risk and offer me a place on the course. They would, however, expect me to devote as much time as possible to regaining a decent level of sight-reading skills and I would, of course, have to do this in my own time and at my own expense. I was completely thrilled. I was desperate to start training and would have agreed to anything. Two years later, at my award ceremony, the same director of music handed me my diploma, with a commendation, and as he leant over to shake my hand he whispered, 'Bloody hell, *that's* a result!'

I had certainly come a long way in those two years and had learnt a great deal but my formal sight-reading skills hadn't improved much at all. To my great delight, I'd discovered that improvisation would be at the heart of much of my work and I'd found a place of musical comfort very early on in my training. In the five years that had followed, the focus of most of my clinical work was in hospices where I worked with people who were often coming to music for the first time. I'd needed to take a broad and flexible approach to working creatively and, as a result, my relationship with music had changed and developed in all sorts of new ways. There was, however, always the nagging worry at the back of my mind that one day my Brahms $C^{\#}$ minor moment would come back to haunt me and I would find myself staring hopelessly at the music, my fraud revealed. When Diana arrived as a new patient at the hospice I couldn't help feeling that the moment had finally come and that the game was up.

Diana was 72 years old and was suffering from the advanced stages of COPD (chronic obstructive pulmonary disease). She was also an extraordinarily gifted pianist. I'd been sitting in the music room looking ponderously at her referral form for about ten minutes, my eyes repeatedly drawn to the Reasons for Referral column. *All-round love of music*, it said. *Read music at Cambridge; classically trained concert pianist.* The truth was I already knew some of this because Diana was in the day centre playing the piano—Chopin —brilliantly, and all of the doors had been opened so that the music could drift down the corridors and out into the gardens. It was exquisite. There was one other sentence on the referral form that had also held my attention for some time. *Diana,* it said, *is also a psychotherapist.* I took a long deep breath and went to collect her from the day centre.

Diana arrived at our first session looking angry. Having listened to her play for the last fifteen minutes, I'd imagined that she would drift serenely across the garden and I was surprised at how prickly she felt.

'Welcome to the music room, Diana,' I said.

'Di,' she replied, 'please call me Di. No one calls me Diana.'

'Of course. Sorry. It's good to meet you. How are you?'

'How *am* I?' She let out a long sigh of frustration, her chest wheezing as she breathed. In an instant she looked incredibly sad. 'Well, bloody awful actually. Look…at these…bloody things.' She held out her hands in front of me, both of them trembling. 'Oh, I'm sorry, really bloody sorry. I didn't mean to come in here and just start moaning straight away.'

'It's okay to moan, Di. Is this something new…with your hands, I mean?'

'No, not really. I've had the bloody wobbles for ages but recently I think they're starting to get worse.' We sat quietly for a moment, two musicians thinking about hands and fingers. Was she waiting for me to ask the obvious question, I wondered.

'I heard you playing; it was wonderful.'

'Thank you. You are kind.' And immediately she began to cry. I'd had all sorts of fantasies about how this first meeting might go with Diana but none of them had been remotely like this. I was about to offer some words of comfort when she stole the moment from me. 'I'm sorry, shall we start again? I'm Di. I play the piano…and I'm not normally this horrid, or emotional…well, sometimes…maybe. I've been *so* looking forward to meeting you.'

I smiled back at her. 'Thank you, Di. I've been looking forward to meeting you, too. How can I help?'

'You could relax a little,' she said and I laughed out loud as she smiled back at me.

'I'm sorry. I didn't realise that I was…' I was groping for a word but she didn't let me finish the sentence:

'Well, you do seem a little tense. I know I'm an ogre but I promise I won't bite your head off. Well, not every session, anyway.'

'Thanks, Di. I'd appreciate that.' We were both laughing now.

'I know that look, you know,' she said.

'Look?' I asked.

'Yes, *that* look,' she said, widening her eyes as she stared at me. 'The "Oh, my God, the client from hell" look.'

'That's a little unfair isn't it?' I replied, still smiling.

'Maybe, a little, but,' she chuckled and shrugged her shoulders, 'I *definitely* wouldn't want *me* as a client. So, I do understand.'

'What do you mean, Di?' I thought I knew what she was referring to but I wanted her to say it. I certainly wasn't prepared for her reply.

'Well, you know, an alcoholic, a history of manic behaviour and suicide attempts and now, mostly just…rage.' She paused and looked over at me. 'You look a little surprised.'

'Well,' I said, 'I guess I was expecting you to say something different—about you being a psychotherapist—something like that but…'

'And a musician too?' she interrupted.

'Well, yes, that too. Do you want to talk about the rage or would you rather just play?'

'I'll save the rage for later. What would you like to hear?'

'You choose, Di,' I replied.

'Some Debussy then.' She stretched out her fingers and laid her hands gently on top of the piano keys. 'Bloody wobbles,' she said and began to play.

I sat and listened to the beautiful piano meditation, *Rêverie*, and watched Diana's hands glide confidently over the keys. Despite the slight trembling, she played elegantly; her touch was incredible, one of the most graceful things I'd ever seen.

'Thank you, Di, that was beautiful.' I sat and waited for a little while until I realised that Di was crying again; silent tears that rolled off her face onto her arms, which were folded tightly across her chest. We both sat with the silence until she eventually spoke.

'I was in hospital, just a few weeks ago. I'd been having some… soul dreams, I'll call them, and I woke up in the middle of the night surrounded by people who were very sick— someone was dying actually—and I thought, "No, I can't do this; it's not my time. I'm too angry to die". That's why I'm here; that's why I asked to see you.'

Before I could respond, she turned back to the piano and started to play again. Chopin this time, the piece I'd heard drifting through the garden. There were more fireworks in this performance and I noticed that Di would occasionally become very breathless. But despite this she played beautifully and I couldn't help being completely drawn in to the music.

'Beautiful,' I said when the music was over. 'You were a concert pianist, I believe?'

'Yes, briefly. But an accompanist mostly, for many years, after I'd started playing again.'

'You stopped playing?'

'Yes, for a while. In my 30s.' I sat and waited. 'You're going to ask me why, aren't you?'

'That was…sort of going to be my next question, Di.'

'Drink…despair…and too many broken bones,' she replied and before the final words had left her lips, she'd turned to the piano and started to play again.

Definitely not the first session I'd imagined, I wrote in my journal after she'd left. *You're not kidding,* I thought to myself; *not even remotely close.*

On the way to the music room for our next session, we walked through the garden, Diana holding my arm. 'I've heard that you help people to write songs,' she said.

'Yes, lots of people here have written them with me.'

'My grandson's a songwriter, plays bass in a band, too. They're very good, well, he's brilliant really. He's just started studying music, you know, one of the contemporary courses. He's doing very well. Absolutely loves it.'

'You studied at Cambridge, didn't you? That must've been great?'

'Yes, best days of my life. I adored it there.' We'd arrived in the music room and Diana had taken her seat at the piano.

'How are your hands today?' I asked.

'Still got the wobbles but they're not aching so much. I haven't played my piano at home all week and I think that's helped a bit. Well, it's helped my hands but it hasn't done much for my state of mind.'

'I'm sorry,' I replied. 'Would you like to play something now? Together perhaps?'

'Yes, on the piano?'

I looked over at my guitar, longingly. 'Yes,' I replied, my heart sinking. 'If you like.' I took my place at the lower end of the piano and whispered a silent prayer.

'What's your favourite key?' she asked.

'F, and, as you're about to discover, it's pretty much the only key I can play in.'

She looked at me and giggled playfully. 'Brilliant! I *love* F!'

There were so many things that could have gone wrong at this moment but Diana made sure that they didn't. I began to play a couple of chords and she mirrored them, adding a few grace notes here and there, and we began to develop a cheerful musical theme. The more we played, the more my confidence grew and eventually I started to relax and enjoy the experience of playing alongside her. At one point I became acutely aware of her almost ethereal therapeutic presence, holding me in the music, making me feel safe. I knew that I was supposed to be the therapist in this relationship but I allowed myself the luxury of being healed, free from self-criticism and judgment for those few minutes. It felt wonderful; the mask was off and I seemed to be surviving.

'Thank you, Di. That was great.' We were smiling at each other, Di massaging her fingers.

'Thank you, Bob. It *was* great. We can get on with it now, can't we?' she said, and we both knew exactly what she meant.

Diana was born in 1935 and was an only child. When she was five or six years old, her mother became ill. Diana remembered this time vividly, sitting on her mother's bed waiting for her to wake up and play with her, the darkness of the room—curtains drawn, the pallid shade of her mother's skin, the whispered voices outside the door and the lingering smell of sickness and her father's cigarettes. Diana was never told when her mother had died. She was collected from school by friends of the family who lived a few miles away and she didn't return home to her father for several months. She didn't attend the funeral and no one ever spoke of her mother's death. Diana had adored her mother and couldn't believe that she could just disappear like that. She was heartbroken and furious.

As she grew up, she tried to talk to her father about what had happened but he remained adamant that it had been in her best interest to have been excluded, both physically and emotionally. He couldn't understand why, after all these years, it should be so important to her, as if suddenly losing the one person who made your world safe wasn't going to be a complete catastrophe; especially when no one had told you how, or why.

Diana began to experience long periods of depression, anger and self-loathing. Her anger would often turn into an uncontrollable rage; she had suicidal ideations and started to self-harm. She married in her twenties and had two children but the marriage had ended unhappily and she began to drink excessively. By the time she was 30, she was an alcoholic, divorced and living alone. She had become, in her own words, worthless. Over the six years that followed, she became a familiar patient at Accident and Emergency departments and was admitted to hospital on over twenty occasions. Some of these admissions resulted from accidental injuries when she'd been drunk but four of them were due to serious suicide attempts. Her fourth and final attempt had been a leap from the fifth floor of an office building. She broke her back, both legs and feet and shattered her pelvis; it had been a miracle that she'd survived at all.

'It's a long time since I've talked about this with anyone,' she said. I'd been listening to Diana for the last 30 minutes. It was our third session and I'd asked her about the comment she'd made when I'd quizzed her about not playing the piano. Drink, despair and broken bones; the words had stayed with me, and what I'd heard had shocked me.

'How did you survive that last attempt?' I asked. 'What happened to you?' I'd got used to hearing all sorts of stories in the therapy room and I was beginning to try to equate this particular shocking history with the woman who was sitting beside me. I thought of the way that she walked, the stoop in her posture, and the way she kicked her foot inwards, awkwardly sometimes. I tried to imagine her as a young woman, flying through the air, crash-landing, hoping to die.

'Well, I was unconscious for a few days, I think. When I eventually woke up, I was on a ward with lots of other people but no one spoke to me. There were lots of filthy looks but no conversations. I remember one of the doctors in particular; I told him I needed to go home. "Please," I said, "my children need me." He looked at me with utter contempt and replied, "Well you certainly didn't give *them* a thought when you chucked yourself out of the window, did you?" Of course, that wasn't true but I couldn't tell him. I felt so worthless; I didn't have the right to say anything at all. In the end, when they could move me, I was transferred to a psychiatric hospital and that was such a relief. I can't begin to tell you what was going through my mind while I was stuck on that general ward. They were the darkest days of my life, absolutely, the darkest days. No one was going to come *anywhere* near my despair or try to give me back even the tiniest shred of dignity. I was drowning in my helplessness and that just seemed to make them even more angry with me. I don't think I've ever wanted to be more...*dead*...than I did on that ward.'

We sat quietly. It had started raining and the day centre staff were rushing past the window, gathering up the cushions and the chairs.

'There was one particular dream that I've never forgotten,' she continued, 'a death dream, I think. I was...skimming along...you know, in space. There was this enormous spaceship full of people; I could see them through the windows and I kept banging on the door and shouting to them to look because I was out there, sitting on a rainbow, swinging my legs, finally free. But none of them noticed me; they just stared straight ahead, empty, like they had nothing to believe in. I banged and I screamed but it never made any difference.'

'That's a powerful image, Di.'

'Yes, it's certainly stayed with me.'

'Could almost be a song, don't you think?'

'If you say so. Come on then; show me how to do it.'

It took about half an hour to write 'Skimming Along'. For someone who professed to have no songwriting skills, Diana was a natural lyricist.

Skimming Along

Skimming along, skimming along, skimming along over rainbows
Knocking so hard on the door of a spaceship,
Wondering whether they'd see me
...But
None of them saw me, safe on my rainbow, swinging my legs as I
watched them
Yet I'm free and I'm happy with wonderful views
Of the planet beneath me, the forests and pastures and oceans so blue
...So
I'll settle for space and the beautiful rainbows
And the stars which surround me and hold me in truth

The melody was complex. Diana wanted to use several different time signatures and three or four key changes. This was certainly not the standard songwriting format that I was used to but I found myself relishing the challenge. The recording of the song, our first together, reveals us both tentatively negotiating our way through the arrangement. At one point on the recording, Diana whispers, 'Where to now?' to which I reply, 'G...I think.' If this was going to be my Brahms $C^{\#}$ minor moment, I'd happily take it, anytime. She was delighted with the results and took the CD home to play to her friends. I was aware that we'd stopped to write the song at what had been a significant moment in our conversation and I wondered if this had been a mistake. However, I needn't have worried. Diana, I was learning, would grace all of our sessions with her very human, reflective, insightful presence. She was very clear about why she was coming to see me and she was also delighted to allow me to lead the way sometimes. At our next session, I asked if we could pick up the story again and she agreed.

Diana was a patient in the psychiatric hospital for ten months and it was here that she believed her life had been truly saved. A young psychiatrist had taken a particular interest in her case and they'd spent many hours together. I asked her what it was about this particular young man and she said, 'He knew right at the beginning how vulnerable I was. I'd arrived at the point where there was *nothing* about me that had any value at all. I was utterly worthless; well, at least that's how I felt. I'd lost everything— my children, my marriage, self-respect — all gone. I wasn't playing a single note of music. In truth I was so drunk most of the time that I couldn't have played even if I'd wanted to. I truly, truly *hated* myself.

'And then, in walked this man, holding all the cards, of course, and you know what it's like in these situations. Sometimes people, professionals, can make you feel so...*powerless*. But he didn't; he took his time and he was kind, you know, genuinely kind. It was more than empathy; he was compassionate and I started to believe that he *did* care about me. And that's what made all the difference; that's when things started to change. It was my first experience of *good* therapy and it saved my life. I've absolutely no doubt about it. It's what made me want to become a therapist myself. He was creative, too, a bit like you, although we never did any music together. He'd bring me poems and other little bits of writing; inspirations, I suppose. I've kept them all. One of them,' she paused in an attempt to control her emotions, 'one of them is called Hope, H, O, P, E—Hold On, Pain Ends.'

Diana had started to cry and she reached over and took my hand in hers, gripping it tightly. 'Never be afraid to love your clients Bob; love can save lives...d'you know what I mean?'

'I think so,' I replied, 'I think so.'

Diana was smiling through her tears. 'Bloody hell! I really *am* the client from hell, aren't I?'

I laughed out loud. 'No! Not at all. It's incredibly helpful to hear you talking like this; hope is such a powerful thing, isn't it?'

'That's for sure,' she replied. 'Sometimes, for some of us, it's the *only* thing.'

By the time Diana was discharged from the psychiatric hospital, she'd decided that she would never again attempt to kill herself.

'Even if *I* wasn't worthy of that decision,' she said to me, '*he* was. He helped me to save my own life and I could never, *ever*, dream of burdening him with my death.'

Within a few months, she'd joined Alcoholics Anonymous and had stopped drinking. I knew from reading her notes that Diana held a position of some responsibility with AA. Before I could mention it, she'd turned to the piano and started noodling, which was her word for improvising, and, as I came to learn eventually, was often a sign that she was plotting something.

'You know I told you about James, my grandson?'

'Yes,' I replied, 'the bass player.'

'That's him. Well, it's his birthday coming up; he's going to be 21 and I thought it would be great if I could write him a birthday song. What do you think?'

'Sounds great, Di. What sort of thing do you have in mind?'

'Ah, ha!' she said, giggling to herself, 'I have a cunning plan!'

Diana's plan was brilliant. She'd been teaching James to play the Bach Prelude and Fugue in C major from *The Well-Tempered Clavier* and he'd recently been showing her, rather proudly, how he'd mastered the piece. Anyone who has taken even rudimentary piano lessons will almost certainly be familiar with this particular piece of music; it's a challenge to learn but incredibly satisfying to play.

'So,' she said, 'I'll play the Bach and write the words; you sing them.'

'It sounds great, Di,' I said, 'er…there are a lot of notes, aren't there?' I was trying to imagine how many hundreds of words she would need to write to match the music and how, indeed, I might even begin to try to sing them.

'That's the *cunning* bit of the plan,' she said. 'You can write a new melody. It'll be me, you and J. S. Bach. Just imagine, the dream team!' She reached over and placed her hand on my shoulder, shaking it gently and said, 'This…is going to be great fun,' then turned back to the piano and began playing.

Sometimes, when I listen to the recording of this song, I find it hard to believe that I was actually in the room at all. It was such an extraordinary experience. As Diana played the prelude, she simultaneously began calling out the words and I scribbled them down as fast as I could, struggling to keep up. There was hardly a pause in the process other than at the very end when she stopped to consider the words for a moment.

'It's okay,' she said, 'I'm not stuck. I'm just trying to find the right way to tell him that we don't always have to fly away in order to find love.'

'Maybe you could just remind him to come home from time to time,' I said with a smile on my face.

'Perfect,' she replied, 'let's do that.'

Song for James

On the day that you were born, you came from darkness into light
How strange it must have been, how strange
I was pacing on the floor, listening for the phone
To tell me you were here, safe into the world

Safe into the world, at last. Safe into the world

From a baby to a boy, from a boy into a man
I have watched you grow, I've watched you fly, fly, fly
And though I know that's how you dream
Remember
Your dreams can lead you home

We made no attempt to compose the melody formally. Instead I set up the microphone at the end of the room by the piano, placed the hastily scribbled words on a stand in front of us and sang whatever notes came into my head.

'There,' she said when we'd finished our one and only take, 'I knew you could do it. Johann Sebastian would *love* this.'

Being with Diana in these creative moments was a little like being in another world. Her musicality was sublime; it fell from her like a beautiful rich liquid and then gently poured itself back into everything that she touched, including me.

'Well,' I said, 'I've got no idea where that came from.'

'Good,' she replied. 'It doesn't do to worry about these things too much; best left with the gods, don't you think?' And, of course she was right.

There was a very practical side to Diana; she loved unpicking things, trying to understand structures and processes, particularly those present in human relationships. 'We have to keep listening and searching to be responsive,' she said to me. But at the same time, she revelled in mystery and loved being a part of it without having to try to solve it. Her early association with AA and the Twelve Steps introduced her to Eastern philosophies and she adored Rumi, the great Sufi poet. 'Remember Rumi,' she'd say to me when I appeared to be struggling. 'There are more than a hundred ways to kneel and kiss the earth.'

GRACE: PART TWO

As the months wore on, Diana's health began to deteriorate and she was admitted to the in-patient unit for a few days to try to get her symptoms under control.

'Will you please, for God's sake, take me to the music room!' I'd just stuck my head inside her doorway to see how she was and I knew that this was more of a demand than a request. By the time we'd arrived at the music room and I'd helped her out of the wheelchair, which she utterly despised, Diana was on the verge of tears.

'Don't you dare ask me how I am,' she said.

'That's okay, Di. I wasn't going to,' I replied.

'Because I'm absolutely shit,' she said and we both burst out laughing. I picked up my guitar, sat next to her and started playing the blues.

'Woke up this morning,' I sang.

'Feeling like shit,' she responded. 'I've got the antibiotic effing blues!'

'Do you want to write this?' I asked.

'Oh yes,' she replied. 'Get your pen.'

The Antibiotic Blues

Woke up this morning feeling like shit
Looked in the medicine cabinet decided to take a hit
Cus, baby, I got the antibiotic blues
Don't like feeling like this and the tragedy is
I can't take no more booze

Well there's Horlicks in the cupboard, and the cat is feeling rough
Ain't nothing I can do about it, I hate the rotten stuff
Cus, baby, I got the antibiotic blues
Don't like feeling like this and the tragedy is
I can't take no more booze

Double up on painkillers, paracetamol don't work
Ran out of codeine, baby, I'm going berserk

Well I ain't got no fix, like how I used to mix
I never took 'em one at a time, it was more like five or six
Cus, baby, I got the antibiotic blues
Don't like feeling like this and the tragedy is
I can't take no more booze

I used to take them all the time…with booze

'Well, I hope you're proud of it,' I said after we'd listened through to the recording of the song. 'I think it's great.' The entire process had taken about 30 minutes and Diana was sitting at the recording desk wearing a big pair of studio headphones.

'I want this at my funeral,' she said. 'Will you sing it?'

'Are we ready to start talking about your funeral today, Di?' I asked. She nodded. 'Okay, then yes, of course, as long as I'm still around, I'll sing "The Antibiotic Blues" at your funeral. I'm not sure what the vicar might think though.'

'It's okay; he won't be surprised,' she said and grinned at me. 'You can ask me now, if you like.'

'Okay.' I paused and took a breath. 'How are you, Di?'

'Better,' she said. And her whole face was smiling.

In the days that followed, Diana was a regular visitor to the music room. Sometimes she'd simply want to play the piano but, being resident in the hospice, albeit temporarily, she'd found herself thinking more and more about her future and she wanted to talk about it.

'What do you know about death anxiety?' she asked one afternoon. We'd been playing together and Diana had started to write a song for her daughter.

'Well, I think it's something that all of us experience at some level throughout our lives,' I said. 'We might give it another name at times, or try to explain it away as some or other form of crisis, but, ultimately, we all know we're mortal. We know that we're going to die. I imagine that this has always been a part of your work as a therapist, hasn't it?'

'Yes,' she replied, 'I suppose it has.'

'So, what are you thinking, Di?'

'I'm thinking…' She paused. 'I'm thinking it's starting to feel rather…more real.' We sat quietly for a few moments, letting her words sink in.

'What do you need, Di?' I asked. Diana took her time to answer, looking up and down at the piano, massaging her fingers.

Eventually she replied, 'I don't know. What've you got to give me?'

I smiled back at her. 'Permission, maybe? To do it your way?'

Diana smiled back at me. 'Okay, thank you. I'll take that as a starter,' she said and after a pause added, 'I don't want to bloody die.'

'I know you don't. I don't want you to bloody die either.' We sat looking at each other. 'Come on,' I said, 'you've got a song to finish.'

Di had two children, Jonathan and Sara, and she wanted to create something musical for each of them to celebrate their birthdays. She'd begun to make several pages of notes about Jonathan and we were looking at them together one day when I reminded her that it was

Sara's birthday that came first and that we'd already made a tentative start. 'Shouldn't we be working on Sara's song?' I'd wondered aloud.

'Yes, you're right,' she said, 'but I don't know how to do it. She's awesome…incredible…and she's all of these things despite having me as a mother.' I wanted to interrupt with something positive but she didn't let me. 'I was a bloody *horrible* mother when I was drinking. Can you imagine what it must have been like, for both of them? They're both who they are *despite* having to grow up with a drunk mother like me, and that's pretty incredible, isn't it?' She played a few notes on the piano. I sat and waited for her anger to settle. Her children had become very successful in their chosen professions; I'd met them both and had instantly liked them.

'You fought for them, didn't you, Di? You got them back.'

Diana had told me about the years that followed her final suicide attempt, her involvement with AA and how she'd managed to rebuild her relationship with her children little by little. In the beginning it had felt almost impossible; she was often overwhelmed by feelings of guilt and self-loathing. 'I couldn't expect them to even like me, never mind *love* me,' she'd said. Working as a counsellor with AA had allowed her to understand herself a little more and this in turn had helped her to keep on trying. 'I wasn't about to abandon them again, that's for sure,' she'd said.

'You're right, Bob. I did fight for them. Was that enough though? What could I ever do to make it up to them? I mean, how can you atone for…what I did, for who I was?'

'You know, Di, I wonder if your whole life hasn't been an atonement in some way. Ever since you lost your mother; the horror, the guilt, and blame you had to deal with. But…come on, you know all this stuff; you've been in therapy for 30 years; you've been a therapist yourself for almost as long. In the end you gave them what they needed and what *you* didn't have. A mother to love…and to be loved by.'

'And is that enough?' There were tears in her eyes.

'You know what, Di,' I replied, 'if love isn't enough, then we're all…fucked!' We both burst out laughing; Diana's language had always been colourful but I'd managed to avoid joining in until now.

'You're *charming* when you swear,' she said, grinning broadly.

'Thanks,' I replied, 'shall we get on with it then?'

Diana decided to set 'Sara' to Debussy's *Clair de Lune*, one of her favourite piano pieces and one that Debussy himself had used for the setting of a poem. The song begins with Sara's birth—October girl, she calls her—recalling how she was born just as the harvest moon was rising. She remembers her as a small girl, a water baby, an adventurer, fearless and brave.

'She'd bloody well needed to be with *me* as her mother,' Diana had said as she called out the words to me from the piano and I scribbled them down, suggesting the occasional repeat or revision. The finished song is beautifully crafted. Without leaning on sentimentality at all, it completely captures her love for her daughter and, towards the end, provides her with the opportunity to offer just a little advice: caution comes with wisdom, she says, you can't be brave if you don't know how to be frightened.

Diana's playing on the recording is sublime. I encouraged her to use some of the studio's more modern technology to re-create other instrumental sounds and she revelled in her new-found access to the orchestra. The finished recording oozes with her musicality; it's completely gorgeous. She was justifiably proud of the song and was delighted when she was able to play it to a large assembled crowd at Sara's 50th birthday party.

Sara

Sara, October girl, Sara, October girl
Born after sunset, just as the harvest moon rose

Sara, October girl, mermaid without a tail
So cross at leaving the warm water place

In a hurry as she's always been
Two days early as I knew she'd be
And such an angry bunny

Sara, fearless child, Sara made up her mind
Race to the water, wherever it might be

What a funny girl
Such a faithful girl
Golden girl

Just a little tomboy climbing trees
Slipped out of windows when no one sees
Little miss adventure

Keeps on going when the going gets tough
Like Tina Turner when she struts her stuff
Those brown-eyed looks speak volumes

Caution comes with wisdom
You can't be brave if you have no fear, have no fear, Sara

Sara, October girl
New waters lie ahead

Diana's health continued to deteriorate and her respite visits to the in-patient unit became more frequent. Despite her fiercely independent nature, she was finding these short periods of being cared for very helpful. They also allowed us to spend a little more time together. We'd known each other for over a year now and there was a fluidity to our relationship which felt very comfortable. However, there was the small matter of a therapeutic relationship that I was doing my best to maintain. Diana knew this, of course, but increasingly there were times when my attempts to reinforce some of those boundaries could result in an angry response. On one occasion I'd sent her an email confirming an appointment and, in a quite formal way, thanking her for something she'd recently written. I also made the fatal mistake of beginning my mail with the words, 'Hope this finds you in good spirits.'

She replied immediately and was clearly furious. 'You're going to need a very large crash-helmet! "Good spirits" indeed, when I've got the Hound of the Baskervilles snarling at me in triplicate and I'm tottering like a 95-year-old crock! My hands are so shaky that I'm going to dip them in starch and call myself Morticia! I'm so pissed off at being tired and unmotivated; I can only play very, very sad music. Such detachment! Where have you gone, Bob? Have I moved to another planet? I know I'm not well but PLEASE take the kid gloves off! Best politically correct wishes...from your client from hell.'

I was shocked at first but soon realised that I'd made a stupid mistake. Diana was dying and hating every moment of it. Good spirits, indeed!

It was the following week and Diana was noodling on the piano.

'I've been reading about Tim Burton's new film, *Alice in Wonderland*,' she said.

'Oh yes?'

'Yes,' she said, 'and I'd like to go and see it. Very much.'

'Great, you should.'

'I think you should take me.'

'Sorry?'

'I think you should take me. It's...years since someone took me to the pictures.'

I looked over at Diana and could tell that she was deadly serious.

'Are you asking me for a date night?' I asked, grinning.

She turned and gave me a withering look. 'Huh! Don't push your luck! I just need a driver.'

I duly picked her up later that week and drove her to the cinema. She was very quiet and hardly spoke a word until we were finally seated and the opening credits began to roll. 'Thank you,' she said and slipped her arm into mine, where it stayed for the entire film.

At one point, I became aware that she was crying and whispered to her, 'Are you okay?'

'Yes,' she whispered back, 'just saying goodbye.'

I decided to put on a fundraising concert that would feature some of the songs that clients had written in the five or six years that I'd been working in hospices. A theatre was booked and with the help of a close colleague, Jane, a band was assembled and rehearsals were already underway. I'd had several long conversations with Diana about the concert: Was it okay to share material like this in such a public arena? Would people find it too difficult to listen to? Would they even come? Diana was adamant that it should go ahead and she was very keen to be a part of it. I would have loved to have her play the piano all the way through but we both knew that this wasn't a realistic option anymore. Grudgingly Diana agreed to open the concert with some Debussy and to perform her song for Sara. The date was set for Tuesday 19th April and, despite my early concerns, the tickets sold out. We'd have a full house after all.

In the weeks that followed, Diana and I continued to meet each other regularly and our sessions took on a very different flavour. Diana became far more reflective and spent a great deal of time talking about her past, filling me in on some of the gaps in her history, which, at times, was difficult to hear. Every now and then she'd take my arm and check me out, making sure I was okay.

'You know you're doing *my* job, don't you?' I asked on one occasion.

'Bugger off,' she replied. 'It's *my* death.'

One early spring afternoon, a few weeks before the concert, Diana was sitting at the piano, massaging her fingers. She'd tried to play but it had been too painful. In the past this would usually have led to an outburst of frustration but now she was just sitting quietly, looking out into the garden.

'What are you thinking, Di?'

She took a long time to answer. Eventually she turned to me and said, 'I'm thinking…I've searched for so long for someone to share a bit of my journey with. You know, pain can often lie so deep inside but it can't hide forever, which is why the music we've made has been so important. It's music from my heart, and my soul. It's been my joy… and my pain.' She looked down at her hands and I sat quietly, waiting.

Eventually she looked up again and smiled. 'Grace, that's what I've longed for, what I've searched for all of my life. But it never seemed to find me in the right place. I think I've finally learnt that grace isn't something I could earn; it's something I would have to receive.' She paused again and looked around the room before continuing. 'And this —you, me, this room, the music—maybe this *is* it. Maybe this can be my saving grace.'

I was fighting to control my emotions. 'It feels like we're saying goodbye.'

'Oh, we've always been saying goodbye,' she replied, 'but we've done it beautifully, haven't we?'

Diana died two days later. I'd spoken to her on the phone in the morning and asked if I could see her at home. She'd been adamant about not meeting. I'd finished the recording of her song, 'Grace', and I'd wanted her to hear it.

'Sing me a bit of it,' she'd said and I'd sung the chorus to her over the phone:

Grace, it's what I long for
Grace, it's what I've searched for
It never seemed to find me in the right place
So maybe you can be my saving grace

'Lovely,' she'd said, 'now, go and do some work and don't worry about *me*. I'm fine.' She died at home later that evening with her children by her side.

The family arranged Diana's funeral for 19th April, the date of the concert. Sara wrote to me saying, 'The concert will be lovely and Mum will be enjoying it from wherever she is. No doubt she'll have some suggestions for improvements, too!' At her funeral we sang 'The Antibiotic Blues', albeit a slightly cleaned up version, and the whole ceremony was full of the music that she loved. During the concert that evening, we opened the second half with *Clare de Lune* and saved 'Grace' for our encore. I struggled to sing the song without falling apart; it felt as if Diana was in every note and every word and it brought the house down.

It took me a long time to get used to not seeing Diana every week. In the year and a half that we'd worked together, I'd learnt a considerable amount. Diana had given me the insight and the confidence to try to become the kind of therapist I'd always wanted to be and I knew that it had been one of the most important relationships of my life. I wasn't trying to replace her but, at times, I was guilty of wishing that I could.

Diana's parting gift to me was a song. She'd left a large white envelope with the hospice chaplain with instructions not to pass it on to me until my birthday. On the front she'd written, 'From your nightmare muse. With love.' I sat at the piano and opened the envelope to find a handwritten manuscript of the music, together with a lyric sheet for the song that she'd entitled 'To the End of Time'. With typical playful irony, she'd set the music in the key of C$^{\#}$ minor. It's a very beautiful song, of course. And I can play it all the way through.

RAY

LUNCH

*What lies behind us and lies before us are small matters
compared to what lies within us.
And when we bring what is within out into the world, miracles
happen.*
Henry David Thoreau.

Ray was a poet, a kind and gentle country man. After what he
described as 'a near lifetime' of treatment for abdominal cancer, he'd
begun attending the hospice day centre.

'I'm a survivor,' he said during our first session, 'but even
survivors have to watch the sun go down in the end.'

I warmed to Ray from the moment we met; he was quietly spoken,
charming and good humoured despite being in considerable
discomfort. His referral form had stated that he was looking for an
opportunity to be creative and address 'one or two issues' and during
the session I asked if there was anything in particular that he'd like to
talk about.

'Not really,' he replied, 'not today, anyway. But thank you.'

We started to meet regularly and every week he would arrive at our
sessions armed with his journal which contained the poems and short

stories that he was currently working on. I encouraged him to read his work to me and he seemed to enjoy doing this. On one occasion, about a month into our sessions together, he told me that he'd written a poem about the hospice and was wondering if we might be able to turn it into a song.

'I like the blues, you know,' he said, 'and a bit of country, too. What do you think?'

'Yes,' I replied enthusiastically, 'let's give it a try. What's it called, Ray?'

'Lunch,' he replied, without even a flicker of a smile.

'Lunch?'

'Yeah, you know, here we are in this amazing place, people of all sorts, living, struggling, dying, and, in amongst all of it, there's one thing that you can be absolutely sure of.'

'And what's that, Ray…?'

'That at exactly ten minutes past twelve every day, your lunch will be on the table, ready to eat!'

Lunch

Some days you do, some days you don't
Some days you will, some days you won't
But your lunch is always waiting just the same

Some days you go, some days you stop
Some days you're high, some days you drop
And your lunch is getting dried up just the same

Some days the phone rings, some days not
Some days you catch up but hey, not a lot
And your lunch is sitting spoiling just the same

Some days I wonder if I will starve
Some days my guts growl, it's terribly hard
But your lunch it gets more furry every hour

Here on the treadmill, it's no fun
The walk of life's become a run
Forget about lunch, dream of tea
Home with the feet up, that'll do me

And your lunch is still there waiting just the same

We recorded the song as a slow, country blues with Ray delivering the lines in a deadpan, faux hillbilly voice. He was clearly delighted with the results and left that day with a CD of the song to play to his wife.

When Ray arrived for his session the following week, he wearily lowered himself into a chair and rested his head in his hands. He looked tired and unhappy. I waited, wondering what was on his mind.

'Well, Bob,' he said deliberately, 'I...am a grandad.' It was not what I'd been expecting him to say and he still wasn't smiling.

'Really? Well that's wonderful news. Congratulations, Ray. How is everyone?'

'Yes. Okay, I think, everyone seems to be okay. It's a little girl.'

'Lovely. Have you seen her yet?' I asked.

'No. No, I haven't seen her.' Ray had a look of resignation on his face and it was clear that something wasn't right.

'What's up, Ray?'

He leant back in the chair and crossed his arms. 'Well,' he said, 'the thing is, my son and I had a...what shall we call it...a disagreement. It was stupid, horrible really, something of nothing but...we haven't spoken since. I've tried...but...' He paused, staring into the room at nothing in particular. Eventually, he let out a long sigh and looked over at me. 'Two years, Bob. Imagine that. Two years without speaking to my son. And now he's a father himself.' Ray looked defeated.

'Is there anything that you can do to change it?' I asked. 'Particularly now.'

'Like I said, I've tried. But...oh, you know, he's still very angry with me. He'll see his mum...but not me.'

'So, does this mean you won't be able to see the baby either?'

'I don't think so, not at the moment, anyway.' Ray sighed again and shook his head in silent despair at the situation he found himself in. 'You must think I'm a bit crackers,' he said sadly, looking out at the garden, not making eye contact.

'No, not at all, Ray. I just wish it was different for you; for all of you. Are you sure that you can't— ' but Ray interrupted before I could finish the question.

'I've started to write something for her; a song, well, I think it's a song.'

'Okay, do you have it with you?'

Ray opened his journal, adjusted his glasses and began to read to me. '*Hello to you, my darling, it's good to have you here. We've waited so long for you, now we can raise a cheer…*' Ray stopped and closed his eyes; reading the words was incredibly difficult for him to do. I leant over and placed a hand on his shoulder.

'Shall I read them?'

Ray nodded. 'Yes, please.'

'*It's great to know you made it, one more baby in the land. We can watch you growing bigger, and help you understand.*' A few more words were jotted on the page and what looked like a chorus which I read out in full. '*Mum and Dad are there for you, Mum and Dad are there for you, Mum and Dad are there for you, a lucky baby, tell you true.* It's really beautiful, Ray. I think it'll make a perfect song.'

We sat at the piano together, something we hadn't done before, and I encouraged Ray to play on the white notes and see what sort of melody emerged. He struggled with this at first—he'd always seen himself as a wordsmith more than a musician—but, little by little, he gained confidence and by the end of our session the song had been written and recorded.

'How are you doing, Ray?' I asked as I handed over a CD copy of the song.

'A little better, I think. I'm glad I've done this.'

'It's lovely, Ray. I hope she…they… get to hear it—soon.'

'Me too, Bob,' he said. 'Mc too.'

I found it difficult to imagine quite how awful Ray must have been feeling that afternoon as he left the hospice. Not only was he estranged from his son and unable to visit his new grandchild, he was also actively dying, and all of this was unfolding in what would be the last few months of his life. I'd grown very fond of Ray and sitting listening to the recording of his song had left me feeling terribly sad. *Take this world and if it snores, twist its tail until it roars*, he'd written in the last verse. I sat quietly and wondered who had been at the front of his mind when he'd written those words that afternoon. The granddaughter who he may never meet, or the son who he may never see again? As I wrestled with these feelings in the music room, Ray climbed into the front seat of his volunteer driver Paul's car, still clutching his CD.

Of all the volunteers in the hospice community, the most powerful are likely to be the drivers. They spend their time with patients, often on a one-to-one basis, in an environment where people will regularly tell each other extraordinary things—in cars. Most of the volunteer drivers I've worked with have been highly adept at managing these, sometimes quite intimate, relationships as patients share some of the details from their day as they make their way home. Paul was one such driver, a huge man with a personality to match; everyone loved him.

The following week Ray was laughing with me as he recounted the details of their fateful journey home that day. Paul had noticed that Ray held a CD and asked, 'You been writing songs with our Bob again?'

'Yes, I have,' Ray replied.

'Shall we have a listen then? I loved that last one you did, you know, about lunch. It was great.' Ray reluctantly handed over the CD and they listened to the song together as they began to negotiate the busy city traffic. Paul thought it was beautiful and asked if he could hear it again and Ray had agreed. Paul had, quite naturally, enquired about the new-born baby and Ray, too exhausted to try and hide his feelings, had told him the truth about his relationship with his son. Paul had clearly been touched by the story and said, 'You should give him the CD, Ray.'

'Mmm,' Ray replied, unconvinced.

'No. I mean it,' he said with some determination. 'You should. Where's he live?'

'I can't just go and see him, Paul.'

'No. But we can post it through his letter box, can't we?'

As I listened to the story unfold I was very aware of my contradictory feelings. On the one hand was my uneasiness about a client sharing sensitive work in this way without an opportunity to contextualise it. On the other hand was my sheer delight that the song was on its way to exactly where it belonged.

'You can't say no to a man like Paul, can you, Bob?' asked Ray, grinning. 'Mind you, it's a bloody good job I didn't.' They'd made the detour as Paul had suggested and posted the CD, without any other explanation, through the letter box. Later that evening Ray answered his door bell and was greeted by his son, daughter-in-law and their two-week-old baby.

'It was a bit tense at first, I don't mind telling you,' said Ray, 'but it's getting better, every day. She's really beautiful. My wife calls her Little Miracle and she's dead right about that!'

A month or so later, we put on a concert at the hospice to which everyone was invited. It was a beautiful summer evening and we set everything up outside in the garden in front of the music room. I'd asked some of my clients to perform their songs with me and the garden was packed with patients, their families and friends, staff and volunteers. Ray had become quite frail but was still able to sit with me and deliver a spirited rendition of 'Lunch' which was greeted with rapturous applause and shouts for more. All of his family were there, including Ray's granddaughter who had slept through his entire performance much to Ray's amusement. 'I knew she had good taste,' he said. 'She'll know a good song when she hears one.'

Later that evening as I was packing up the equipment, I felt a tap on my shoulder and turned to be greeted by Paul, the driver. He put his hand on my shoulder and said, 'Good song, that "Lunch".'

'Yes,' I replied. 'It's great, isn't it?'

He looked me straight in the eye and said, 'Other one's better,' and before I could reply, he winked, smiled and walked away. Thank you, Paul.

NEIL

EROICA

You need to let your wounds go down to your heart. Then you can live through them and discover that they will not destroy you. Your heart is greater than your wounds.
Henri Nouwen

I was nervous about meeting Neil. The truth was that I'd already met him many years before at a time when both of our lives had been very different. He'd been responsible for setting up a new contemporary music school in the city and I'd spent a few hours there with him, installing some recording equipment. The meeting hadn't gone too well; he was anxious about the equipment and I'd been in a hurry to get the job done quickly. It had all ended well enough but we hadn't liked each other and seeing his name on the referral sheet and checking out that it genuinely was the same man had made me wonder if we were going to be able to work together.

I saw him sitting in reception reading a magazine and immediately recognised him. He was dressed in jeans and trainers, a black tee shirt, linen jacket and a striped scarf tied in a loose knot. As I approached him, he stood up and smiled.

I was the first to speak. 'Hi, Neil. I'm Bob.' He shook my hand firmly.

'Hi, Bob,' he said, 'good to meet you. So, where are you taking me?'

I looked for a flicker of recognition but saw nothing. As we walked over to the music room, Neil made a couple of remarks about the garden, which looked very beautiful in the late September sunshine. He seemed in good spirits, almost jolly, and by the time we reached my room he was ahead of me.

'Here?' he asked, while at the same time opening the door and letting himself in. 'Wow!' he said, as he looked around. 'This is a surprise. Aren't you the lucky one?'

'Yes, I am,' I said and gestured towards a chair, but Neil had already set his sights on the piano stool and within a few moments he was playing. I sat down and listened as he put the piano through its paces, improvising with great skill and speed, hardly leaving a single key on the piano untouched. It was quite something to be this close to a pianist who played with such ease and flourish and by the time he'd finished I was smiling broadly.

'Yeah, these Yamahas aren't bad, are they; I mean for the money, they do the job?' Neil asked. Slowly he began to return my smile. 'So, what's this music therapy thing?'

I was immediately taken back to our first meeting all those years ago. Why hadn't I liked him then? Perhaps it was because he'd struck me as someone who was fiercely competitive and unwilling to take advice. I'd been installing some small recording studios for the students and there had been a few options to consider, particularly around cabling and the placement of microphones. I'd made a few suggestions which Neil had pretty much dismissed out of hand. He'd made it very clear that he knew his business and that the only way forward was his. I'd offered some tuition on the new machines, which he'd immediately declined and, in the end, I was actively encouraged to leave quickly so that he could get on with things. And here we were together again after fifteen years. I couldn't be sure if he remembered me or not. I had a strong hunch that he did but decided that, for the moment at least, I wouldn't ask him. Instead I replied, 'Yes, this music therapy thing; what had you imagined it might be about?' He was still smiling.

'Good answer,' he said. 'Well, I've been a musician, a professional musician actually, all of my working life. I've been a performer, a composer and a teacher. I've never not *done* music so, where do you want to start?'

Our eyes met briefly before I replied. 'Well, I'm wondering how you are.'

He took a breath, paused and then took another before he replied. 'Shit actually, yeah, really shit.' The smile had left his face and I got my first opportunity simply to sit and observe him for a few moments. His hair, once dark brown, was grey and cropped short. His complexion was pale and his eyes, now they weren't smiling, revealed a weary sadness.

'I'm sorry,' I said, 'this must be a tough time for you.'

'Yeah, it's shit.' There was another long pause before he continued. 'I certainly didn't see this one coming, this…' another pause, '…this cancer business was never on my radar. I mean, I'm not old. I've always taken pretty good care of myself, didn't drink much, never smoked. *Never* smoked.' Another long pause. 'So. Lung cancer. Yeah, it really is shit.'

I'd read through Neil's notes earlier and was aware that he'd been diagnosed with lung cancer just over a year ago. Despite chemotherapy and radiotherapy, the disease had spread rapidly and nowadays he was often in a great deal of discomfort. All active treatment had stopped and he'd been told that his prognosis was very poor. He and his wife had divorced four years ago and the separation had been acrimonious. He was now living with his daughter who had struggled to watch the disintegration of her parents' relationship. She'd emerged as an angry seventeen-year-old who wanted nothing more than her dad to help her through her A levels so that she could go to university to study music and leave home forever. Dad dying of cancer just simply didn't fit into any of her plans and she was refusing to talk about it.

I suddenly found myself feeling incredibly sad and I took a few slow breaths; the intensity of the feelings had arrived without warning. I'd become familiar with some of the challenges that these first encounters can present as clients wrestled with the need to talk honestly and openly, while we therapists did our best to remain objective in the face of what could often feel like distressing and unsolvable detail. *Beware the detail,* I thought to myself. *Stay with the feelings.*

'I'm sorry,' I said again, 'I can't imagine how difficult this must be for you and your family.' I was still breathing slowly in an effort not to betray my emotions.

'Yeah, well,' he said, glancing down at his feet, which were still resting on the piano pedals, 'what can you do?'

I waited and he glanced at me; our eyes met briefly and then he forced a smile onto his face and looked away. Tears were forming in his eyes and I sat silently for a few moments wondering if he might begin to cry. Instead he dabbed at his face with the back of his hand, cleared his throat and asked again, 'What *can* you do?'

Another wave of sadness, and exhaustion, too. I shifted in my chair, rolled my shoulders back to release some of the tension in my neck and asked, 'What would you *like* to do, Neil?'

'My God,' he said, 'now that is one hell of a question!'

One of the things I've come to know about myself is that feelings of exhaustion are often my first response to being confronted with helplessness. I find it difficult to separate these feelings at times, often greeting them like unwelcome enemies more than insightful friends. I wanted to help Neil and I needed to focus my attention and recover some of my energy. Why wouldn't Neil consider his predicament to be anything other than helpless? He was young and in his mind certainly too young to be dying in this way and at this time.

And then there were Neil's unfulfilled ambitions. He was a brilliant musician and all of his life he'd dreamt of a career as a jazz pianist, a performer and a composer. But instead he'd struggled to make a living as a jobbing musician, working in cabaret bands touring the working men's clubs and pubs of Britain, often supporting what he described as 'dreadful, appalling, cheesy comedians'. In the last couple of years, he'd begun to compose more music and had finally secured his first professional commission just weeks before he was diagnosed with cancer. His father had been a successful musician and Neil confessed that one of his greatest regrets was that he'd never been able to make his father proud of him. I'd asked him questions such as 'What were your father's expectations?' and 'Are you sure he wasn't proud of you anyway?' but Neil had remained adamant throughout. His father had set the bar very high and Neil had let him down.

Neil and I were now meeting once a week and our sessions had begun to take on a fairly regular shape. He would start by playing the piano, improvising with all the flourish and skill I'd become familiar with while I sat beside him and listened. This would open up the opportunity for us to talk and we'd spend the next few minutes catching up on how things were for him, practical issues around treatment, pain and symptom management and an update on how things were progressing at home. At this point I would suggest that we played some music together and I would usually reach for my guitar and invite Neil to begin a new improvisation. It was always at this point that things would change.

At first I thought that it might be unfamiliarity with this form of improvisation that made Neil reluctant to enter into it with anything like the commitment he showed when he played alone. I also wondered if it could be something about the way that I was playing that was making him feel restricted in some way; I'm a confident improviser on guitar but certainly no jazz virtuoso. Over the weeks I'd gently probed and wondered aloud why it felt difficult for us to connect in the music. Usually Neil would greet my musings and questions with a smile and a shrug but we were both aware that there was something at play here and neither of us was naming it.

I asked myself several questions about my abilities as a musician and as a therapist. I also wondered about our meeting many years earlier and whether these current difficulties were in some way a manifestation of what had happened then. During one particular session, I decided to jump in with both feet and ask the question that had been on my lips for many weeks. 'Neil, do you remember meeting me about fifteen years ago when you were setting up the new music school at the college?'

'What, the contemporary music course?' he replied.

'Yes,' I said. 'I came over one day to install some of the recording equipment.'

He gave me a long, quizzical look. 'I'm sorry, Bob. I don't remember that at all. Are you sure it was me you met?'

This was certainly not the answer I'd anticipated and I was pretty sure that he was telling me the truth. I stumbled to form a reply. 'Er... yes, I'm pretty sure it was you I met that day but it's not a problem, I er—'

But Neil interrupted to save me. 'Sorry, Bob, for not remembering you. Why did you bring it up now?'

It was, of course, a brilliant question and one that I needed to answer honestly and carefully. 'It feels like we're finding it difficult to play music together. You're such an amazing musician, Neil, so able and skilful, and I'm trying to understand what's behind the tension I'm feeling.'

Neil looked away and sat quietly for a moment before he replied. 'You're just too emotional, Bob.'

My response was as much of a question as it was an apology. 'I'm sorry? Too emotional?'

'No, don't be sorry,' he replied. 'It's not your fault. I just can't deal with...*it*.'

'What's the *it*, Neil? What can't you deal with?'

He reached out and placed his hand on my arm. This was the first time, other than when we shook hands, that there had been any physical contact between us and it felt challenging.

'Look,' he said, 'when you play music, it sounds...emotional...and it feels emotional...and I know that if I join in properly with you, I'm just going to fall apart. And I don't want to fall apart. I don't want to start crying. I just need to be strong...for everyone.'

'I think you are strong,' I replied, 'and crying isn't going to change that.' He removed his hand from my arm and sat quietly looking at the piano keys. Eventually I broke the silence. 'When was the last time you cried, Neil?'

He shrugged his shoulders and shook his head from side to side. I waited. He leant forward in his chair, his arms held tightly across his chest.

'What, proper cried?'

'Yes, proper cried.'

'That would be...*Eroica*,' he said, still looking down at the piano.

'*Eroica.*'

'Yes,' he said. 'Beethoven, Symphony No. 3, the second movement...' He paused and let out a long sigh. 'That second movement, the adagio. It completely breaks my heart.'

'Do you know why?' I asked.

'Well,' he replied, 'I guess it's a lot of things. It's an amazing piece of music, phenomenally brilliant and...and it has all sorts of associations with me and my life.' I tilted my head inquisitively but before I could ask the question, he stopped me. 'No,' he said, 'no, really. I can't go near any of this stuff. Not today.'

We were almost out of time and this felt like a very difficult place to end the session.

'I wonder,' I said, 'how it might be if we sat and listened to *Eroica* together in our next session. How would you feel about that?'

He turned and looked me full in the face and smiled. 'Are you pushing me?' he asked.

'I think I might be,' I replied and smiled back at him.

'Okay,' he said, 'let me think about it. I'll let you know next week.'

We walked together across the garden and as I turned to shake hands, he reached out and put an arm around my shoulders. 'Thanks, Bob,' he said. 'I promise I'll think about *Eroica*.'

'Me too,' I replied.

I had a few minutes to spare before my next client was due to arrive and sat quietly looking at the portrait of Beethoven which hung on the far wall of the music room and which had been a gift from a client several years earlier. She, too, had been a pianist and her love of Beethoven's music, particularly the piano sonatas, had been, in her words, 'the main reason I'm not ready to die yet'. It was hard to look at the portrait without thinking of her but today my head was full of Neil, perching precariously on the thin ledge between life and death, holding onto his emotions for fear that letting go might be the very thing that destroyed him. I wondered what it might be that could be wrapped up so tightly inside and yet so easily unravelled by this piece of music. I checked my music library to make sure that I had a copy of the adagio and in that moment I decided that I wouldn't listen to it until Neil was in the room with me. I had a strong sense that, should he agree to our plan, I would need to be prepared to listen to the music as if I was hearing it for the first time.

Neil failed to show up for our next session. I'd prepared the room, anticipating that we might listen to the adagio together, arranging the chairs in front of my studio speakers, keen to make the experience as rich as possible. I'd selected the recording by The Berlin Symphony Orchestra with Daniel Barenboim conducting, a recording that I'd never heard. I had a nagging thought that Neil had never missed an appointment before and I began to wonder if I'd simply pushed him too far. I waited until lunchtime before deciding to call him at home. The phone was answered after the first ring by a female voice that I initially assumed belonged to his daughter. I introduced myself and she replied, 'Hi, Bob. I'm Maria, Neil's wife...well...ex-wife actually. Neil's told me all about you.'

This was surprising. I knew that Maria lived several hundred miles away and that there had been little or no contact between them for over a year. I prepared myself for bad news.

'Hi, Maria,' I said. 'I was expecting to see Neil this morning and I was wondering if everything is okay?'

'Oh, sorry, Bob,' she replied. 'It's all been a bit crazy for the last few days. Neil had a real dip; he was in a lot of pain and was admitted to oncology at the weekend. But he seems quite a bit better and we think he'll be able to come home tomorrow. I'm so sorry. We should've let you know.'

'No, no,' I replied, 'it's not a problem at all. I'm just pleased to hear that he's feeling a little better. Do you think he'd mind if I popped over to see him?'

'No,' she said, 'I don't think he'd mind at all. I think he'd probably really like that.'

We exchanged a little polite conversation. Maria was friendly and talking together felt comfortable and easy. Not, perhaps, what I might have expected at all. I sat back in my chair and looked over at Beethoven, wondering.

I finished my last session that evening and decided to drop in on Neil before I went home. I found him in one of the patient bays on the oncology ward, sitting upright, reading. He looked tired and was visibly thinner than he'd been just a week earlier when he'd last attended music therapy. I greeted him and he returned my smile; he didn't look at all surprised to see me and I assumed that Maria had let him know that I was planning to visit.

'How are you doing?' I asked.

'Shit,' he replied, 'but I always say that, don't I?'

'Well,' I said, 'it certainly sounds like you've been having a pretty shitty time. Maria mentioned that you might be going home tomorrow.'

'Yeah, it looks like I can go home as long as they can control the pain for me.'

'You okay with all of that?'

'Yeah,' he replied, 'feels safer now that Maria's there.'

'Good,' I said, 'that's really good.'

There were several questions in my mind about home and Maria but this certainly wasn't the time to ask them. It seemed to me that Neil was feeling comfortable with the idea of Maria being around and right now that felt by far the most important thing.

'What are you reading?' I asked as I peered down at the book lying open on his knees.

'*From Darwin to Behaviourism*,' he replied. 'I'm trying to figure out what to think about God and heaven and an afterlife, that kind of stuff.'

I smiled and asked, 'Is it helping?'

'Well, yeah, it is in a way. There's a lot of stuff on classical conditioning, how we respond to things, you know, what we set ourselves up for in life.'

I smiled again. 'So…what have you decided?'

'Well, it's pretty straightforward, Bob,' he replied. 'I figure I can afford not to believe in anything because when I die, if there's no heaven or "land of souls"'—he said these words with some sarcasm —'only nothingness, then I won't know anything about it and it simply won't matter. And if there *is* an afterlife, then I get to go "Good grief, what a result". It's a sort of Pascal's wager, only in reverse. A win-win situation as far as I can tell.'

We laughed together and I said, 'Great, well that's sorted then.'

I left shortly after this exchange, having agreed a time to meet the following week, all being well. Neither of us mentioned *Eroica*; things were moving at speed for Neil now and I needed to consider my response.

Eight days later I met Neil in reception. The contrast to our first meeting, just three months earlier, was profound. He was wearing the same jacket and scarf but now they, like the rest of his clothes, hung loosely from his frame. As he rose slowly to greet me, I could see that he was exhausted and our journey across the garden took several minutes as Neil took each step with great care, one hand gripping my arm, the other clutching a walking stick. We took our customary places at the piano and Neil rested his hands on the keys to play.

'An old friend,' he said and I sat back quietly and listened while he played. 'This is incredibly hard.'

His words echoed the thoughts that had been going through my mind. It was hard because he'd lost some of his amazing dexterity, and harder still because he simply didn't have the energy to engage his extraordinary skills in the way that he could have done just a few weeks ago. But perhaps the hardest thing of all was the way that the piano, his 'old friend', had become the mirror to everything that he'd lost.

'I don't think I want to play,' he said and I looked into his eyes and nodded.

'Of course, what would you like to do, Neil?'

A part of me was expecting him to suggest that we bring the session to an early close, but instead he said, 'Shall we listen to something?'

'Of course,' I replied. 'What would you like to hear?'

He sat quietly for a few moments and then looked at me. Tears were already forming in his eyes. '*Eroica*, the adagio,' he replied.

I looked over at Neil and once again the sadness swept in. What was it about this man, I wondered? What was it about us?

'You sure that's what you want?' I asked.

'Yes,' he replied, 'absolutely sure.'

I tried to keep the experience as informal as possible and suggested that we stayed in our usual seats at the piano while we listened. As the music began to play, I touched Neil on the arm and asked if he was okay.

'Yes,' he replied. 'I'm good.'

Within a few moments, tears began to roll down his face and I watched as he closed his eyes and clasped his hands together tightly in his lap. Soon his shoulders began to shake and he let out a sob, followed by a gasp for breath and then another sob. I sat close by his side, resisting the temptation to reach for a hand or an arm, and soon he began to cry uncontrollably.

'It's okay, Neil. It's okay.'

Eventually he began to take some slow, deliberate breaths and I handed him some water. He took a few sips and then said, 'It's that bloody picture, the album cover.'

'The album cover?'

'Yeah, this album, *Eroica*.'

Neil began to rock slowly backwards and forwards in his chair, his hands still clenched tightly in his lap. 'It's the one my dad bought for me for my birthday. I was about thirteen. There's a picture on the front of the album cover, a jagged rock in the middle of the sea. Well, a vast ocean really, and the waves are crashing all around the rock. It's a wild storm.'

The adagio continued to build as Neil rocked backwards and

forwards in his chair. 'There's a man…stranded on the rock,' he said, struggling to control his breathing. 'He's reaching out; he's all alone. He's screaming out but no one can hear him. Nobody can see him. He's totally abandoned. Lost.' He was shouting through his tears now.

'Who's the man, Neil?' I asked.

He waited, trying to control his breathing enough to reply. 'It's me,' he said, and in that moment it felt as if he'd finally owned up to 40 years of anger, disappointment and loneliness.

The hour that followed the *Eroica* experience would be the last time that Neil and I were together in the music room. I'd made some tea and Neil had begun to tell me about his early childhood, growing up with a father who was fiercely competitive and who demanded the same from his only son. He recalled hours and hours of seemingly endless piano lessons and practice in an effort to become the musician his father demanded he should be, and he described the loneliness and isolation he experienced as a result. Neil told me that the demands he placed upon himself increased at an alarming rate, matched only by his growing frustration and despair at his lack of commercial success.

He began to grow accustomed to being told that he was a brilliant musician and that there was something wrong with a world that simply refused to honour his gifts. This had only fuelled his sense of anger and failure and by the time he reached his 30s he wasn't talking to anyone about any of it. The more he internalised his feelings, the more unwell he felt and the more he began to loathe himself and his life. He stopped listening to the voices around him. Expressions of love and admiration arrived like poison arrows and so he did not attempt to hear them at all. I began to understand a little more about the man I'd met fifteen years ago at the college in the city and why the meeting had felt so difficult for him, and for me.

He talked tenderly about Maria, recalling some of her attempts to reach him, even after they'd divorced, and reflected on his brutal regime of resistance and isolation. One night Maria had walked three miles through deep snow to see him; she was worried about him and had wanted to see if she could help. He wouldn't let her through the door and she'd asked him if there was anyone else in his life. He'd replied, 'Maria, there's no one at all in my life, anywhere,' and she'd left in tears to walk the three cold miles home.

When Neil had seen the image of the man on the rocks, a man about to die, fearful and completely alone, he realised he was looking at himself. The emotional and psychological connection of this image to his own *Eroica* album sleeve—the album that his father had handed to him as a child—had been profound and he realised in that moment that all he wanted now was to be rescued, and loved. I wondered if perhaps he'd known this at some level for many years but the difference today was that he was finally ready to give himself permission to receive it.

Neil was admitted to the in-patient unit a few days after our final session. Maria became a constant presence, as did his daughter, and Neil spent the last three weeks of his life surrounded by his family. Neil and Maria became fully reconciled and performed their own private version of a remarriage one evening, complete with witnesses and a glass of champagne.

Maria was always at his side and she told me that when he died, she felt his presence move deeply through her, leaving her with a sense of love and peace that she would hold onto forever.

Neil and I never spoke of *Eroica* again. I've searched everywhere for a copy of the album sleeve but I've never found one. Recently, while looking at the *Beethoven Collection* on the Internet, I found an album cover depicting a wild and raging sea with waves crashing onto a solitary barren rock. But the rock is unoccupied; the lonely man has gone.

EPILOGUE

TONY: THE LAST TO LEAVE

It would be impossible to write a book about life, death and music without writing something about my eldest brother Tony. Tony and I never had an easy relationship; he was five years older than me and we grew up in the 1960s, me with The Beatles and The Stones, Tony with Wagner and Beethoven. He was a gifted musician—he would hate anyone saying that about him—but it was true. Over the years as I worked as a therapist, I came to realise that Tony was something of a savant. He struggled socially, finding it almost impossible to conform to any of the norms that we encouraged him to engage with. Tony was a professional musician for some time but became so troubled and unwell that he began to see playing music as more of an enemy than a friend. However, music itself continued to be his refuge; he had an encyclopaedic knowledge of composers and their works and could identify almost any piece from the first few opening bars. If you caught him on a good day, he could probably identify the orchestra and the conductor as well.

A few years ago, as the result of an accident, Tony became less independent. As the only remaining local family member, it fell to me to provide him with some regular support. By this time we'd also finally managed to find a doctor who could work effectively with him and, with the help of the right medication, Tony had become calmer and more settled. For the first time in our lives, Tony and I were able to spend long periods of time together comfortably. His radio was permanently tuned to Classic FM or Radio 3 and this would often prompt conversations about the music that we loved or, indeed, didn't. His memory was incredible. On one occasion he reminded me about an Arlo Guthrie album that I loved and used to play a lot at home. I'd managed to get him to listen to it and play along with his violin on a couple of occasions. As I reeled off the song titles, Tony sang the words as if he'd been practising them all day; he probably hadn't heard the album for over twenty years.

The last time I saw Tony was a couple of days before I was rushed back into hospital following my bowel cancer surgery. He'd been visiting me at home and had become distressed about how unwell I'd been looking. As he left my house that day, he turned to me, grabbed my arm and said, 'You're not going to die, are you, Bob?'

'No,' I replied, 'of course not, Tony. I'll see you soon.'

In the days that followed, I was treated for sepsis while at the same time Tony developed viral pneumonia. He was rushed into hospital, almost unbelievably into a room just two floors above me and, on the day that I was discharged, he died. The Arlo Guthrie album's final track is 'The Last to Leave' and we'd sung a few of the words together while I made him tea in his flat a couple of months ago, just a few weeks before all of the bombs had started falling. We hadn't seen any of it coming, of course; it was just a song.

One of the extraordinary things about working in palliative care is that we meet people for whom timeframes have become much more visible and clearly defined. The things that we need to do will need to be done—now—and the things that we've left unsaid will need to be said. Perhaps the greatest thing that they teach us is that we shouldn't wait until we're dying before we start to share our truth and our stories and write our songs. I never told Tony how much I loved him. I hope I have now.

MESSAGE FROM THE AUTHOR

I sincerely thank you for reading this book and I hope you enjoyed it. I'd be grateful if you could take a few minutes to leave an Amazon review. I'm happy to answer any questions you may have so do please get in touch with me by:

Email: bob@bobheathmusic.com
Website: www.bobheathmusic.com
Facebook: www.facebook.com/bob.heath.167
LinkedIn: www.linkedin.com/in/bob-heath-b77676120

If you enjoy reading memoirs, I recommend you pop over to Facebook group We Love Memoirs to chat with me and other authors there. www.facebook.com/groups/welovememoirs

ACKNOWLEDGEMENTS

Many people have helped me put this book together and I'm grateful to all of them for their patience and encouragement. In particular I'd like to thank my 'early readers'— Catherine, Geraldine, Phyl, Judith, Jane, Viv, Marina, Julie and Georgina—who, on many occasions, convinced me to keep going when I wondered if I could, or should.

A huge thank you to Martin Diggle, a life-long friend and writer, whose support and insight throughout this entire process have been helpful beyond measure. My sincere thanks also to Ant Press and, in particular, my editor, Jacky Donovan, whose professional guidance and innate capacity for getting inside the stories have been invaluable.

My partner, Ali, has a very special place in this book because she knows the stories and the music almost as well as I do. For over twenty years, I've brought these extraordinary songs home with me and she's welcomed them in with acceptance and love even when, at times, they've been hard to listen to. It's quite impossible to imagine doing any of this without her.

. . .

My special thanks must also go to all of the families who have given me their permission to tell these stories and to share the songs. It was my decision to change names and details to preserve confidentiality. I hope I've been able to safely honour my clients' lives without compromising any of the deep bonds that I know will always exist between them and their families.

Finally, I want to thank my clients themselves. The stories and the songs are theirs, not mine. In sharing something of their journeys, I've been gifted a legacy of hundreds of songs which celebrate and explore living and dying and the human spirit in a completely authentic way. Their lives have touched mine and I've been changed as a result; and for this I will be eternally grateful.

LISTENING LIST

Session recordings and live concert recordings are available on www.bobheathmusic.com.

Live concert musicians: Jim Bateman, Kate Binnie, Bob Heath, Peter Heath, Paul Holmes, Jane Lings, Pete McPhail, Andrc Pysanczyn, Fraser Tilley.

Jonathan:
Skinny Ghost (Bob Heath)

Rick:
A Song for Paddy (session recording)

Alice:
Ein deutsches Requiem (Brahms)
Wildly Blowing Wind (session recording)
Deepest Blue (session recording)
Below the Sea (session recording)

Oskar:
Every Time I See You (session recording)
Souls and Shadows (live concert recording)
When I'm Gone (session recording)
Once in a Lifetime (session recording)
Liva's Lullaby (session recording)
Don't Stop Breathing (session recording)

Eileen:
La, La (session recording)

Teresa:
You Can Call on Me (session recording)

Nicky:
How Lucky We Are (session recording)

Diana:
Skimming Along (session recording)
Song for James (session recording)
Sara (session recording)
Antibiotic Blues (live concert recording)
Grace (live concert recording)

Ray:
Lunch (session recording)
Hello to You, My Darling (session recording)

Neil:
Symphony No. 3 in E ♭ major (*Eroica*), 2nd movement (Beethoven)

Tony:
The Last to Leave (Arlo Guthrie)

LYRICS

A SONG FOR PADDY

An educated man, left to wander in the hills all alone
Lived in a chicken coop, up in the hills which he called his home
And once a month he'd spend his inheritance on beer
Then wander back to the hills alone and disappear
And this is a song for Paddy

A prisoner of war, lost and alone in a foreign land
Taken in by family, given a meal and an open hand
Then from Germany a simple gift arriving at the door
Says 'Thanks for your humanity
This harmonica is yours, it's yours'

And a simple gift can shape a life
A simple act inspire
When Paddy played harmonica to a child
He lit a fire, he lit a fire

From child to a man, stuck in a world where boys don't cry
The harmonica played Paddy's song when the tears stayed dry
His home and his garden became his chicken coop
His wife and his family, his patience and his truth
And the child stayed alive

And a simple gift can shape a life
And a simple act inspire
When Paddy played harmonica to a child
He lit a fire, he lit a fire
And the fire stays alive

WILDLY BLOWING WIND

Wildly blowing wind, the leaves must dance
The night of shadows has not yet begun
And we shall dance before the light has gone
And we shall dance before the light has gone

Green leaves to sharpen clouds on high
The earth is solid underneath my feet
There's now no doorway to the sky
The air is moving and can taste so sweet

Wildly blowing wind, the leaves must dance
The night of shadows has not yet begun
And we shall dance before the light has gone
And we shall dance before the light has gone

Time is so slow, eternity
And nothing seems to turn another page
The midday sun is burnishing
The ewe tree's dreaming in a different age

Wildly blowing wind, the leaves must dance
The night of shadows has not yet begun
And we shall dance before the light has gone
And we shall dance before the light has gone

DEEPEST BLUE

Deepest Blue, Midnight Blue
Floating along in the air
Deepest Blue, Midnight Blue
I keep thinking of you

Deepest Blue, Royal Blue
Shadows on land, sea and sky
Deepest Blue, Indigo Blue
Sometime my dreams will come true

Now there is nowhere else to run
I'll be forever with you, My Deepest Blue

Deepest Blue, Cobalt Blue
Moonlight is silver and grey
Deepest Blue, Cobalt Blue
Lights will now guide me to you

Now there is nowhere else to run
I'll be forever with you, My Deepest Blue

My Midnight Blue, My Royal Blue, My Indigo Blue
My Deepest Blue

BELOW THE SEA

In the dark and icy water, how long have I been here
Just holding on to a piece of wood in waves of salty fear

The stars I thought were lit with hope have emptied out their shine
The ocean bed is full of ships and one of them was mine, mine

All that was dear to me down below the sea
I cannot hold my piece of wood when life abandons me

There was no lifeboat near me though the voices seemed so close
The oarsmen were just phantoms made of all my fragile hope, my hope

All that was dear to me down below the sea
I cannot hold my piece of wood when life abandons me

All that was dear to me down below the sea
I cannot hold my piece of wood when life abandons me

EVERYTIME I SEE YOU

Everytime I See You, Everytime I'm near you
I get this funny feeling that I could make the day

My mind keeps on telling me, sit down and wait and see
But there has to be another way and it goes straight through the heart

It seems that it's a cruel world, but my love for you is true, my girl
If you have to make the choice for your life make it fast and let
me know

Everytime I See You, Everytime I'm near you
I get this funny feeling that I could make the day

Everytime I See You, Everytime I'm near you
Everytime I See You, Everytime I'm near you
It goes straight through the heart

SOULS AND SHADOWS

Who decides when times are sad
Who decides when times are glad
Should it all feel dark and grey
With memories that fade away

You may think when passing by
I'm up above or in the sky
Please don't be fooled, let's just say
I'll be with you all the way

We are souls and shadows, souls and shadows
You, me and Liva, that will never change
We are souls and shadows, souls and shadows
You, me and Liva will always remain

So now you hear I hope this song
Has found its place where it belongs
And if I hear you sing along
Then you have found where I belong

We are souls and shadows, souls and shadows
You, me and Liva, that will never change
We are souls and shadows, souls and shadows
You, me and Liva will always remain

Should we accept without condition
Should we accept not knowing why
Too many tears, too many questions
What will give us peace of mind

So close your eyes and let us try
Please speak up and don't be shy
I'm asking you to be the one
Who leaves a smile and a bit of sun

We are souls and shadows, souls and shadows
You, me and Liva, that will never change
We are souls and shadows, souls and shadows
You, me and Liva will always remain

You, me and Liva will always remain

———

WHEN I'M GONE

There is a time for tears and crying
There is a time for peace and sleep
But when the night is really over
The dreams are yours to keep

And I see you at night time, I see you at dawn
The things I told you, they came out wrong
I need my own space, I have to let go
And when I'm gone, I'm gone

I might be right, I might be wrong
But when it's written and put in this song
There is no way I could go back again
Back to that place, that place again

There is a time for tears and crying
There is a time for peace and sleep
But when the night is really over
The dreams are yours, yours to keep

And I see you at night time, I see you at dawn
The things I told you, they came out wrong
I need my own space, I have to let go
And when I'm gone, I'm gone

And that's how it's done!

ONCE IN A LIFETIME

I am sad at eleven, bitter at twelve
Angry when I feel it could be nice with some help
Would we have done it any different, would it change a thing
If it happened all over again?

I've been told to die in September sometime
I hate to disappoint, feel like a crime
They're good honest people with decent jobs
And plenty of other things to do

There are no second chances here, you don't get to try again
And even if you did, I wonder if the refrain would be the same
Death only comes once in a lifetime one of these days
You can tell them this, we've chosen to fight, we've chosen to fight

I'd love to arrange a birthday again
Hopefully my daughters, she had it yesterday
We can throw a party, tell them all
We're ready to continue the fight

There are no second chances here, you don't get to try again
And even if you did, I wonder if the refrain would be the same
Death only comes once in a lifetime one of these days
You can tell them this, we've chosen to fight, we've chosen to fight

I am sad at eleven, bitter at twelve
Angry when I feel it could be nice with some help
Would we have done it any different, would it change a thing
If it happened all over again?

LIVA'S LULLABY

When you are in bed, but can't go to sleep
Try closing your eyes and think what to keep
Of all you have seen, we will pick out the best
And find a little thought that will give us some rest

Should bad or evil dreams disturb you in the night
I know it can be tough to keep them out of sight
But I hope that you feel I am holding your hand
Close your precious eyes, sleep as long as you can

But when you wake up and wonder what is true
Lay your hand on your heart, that should give you a clue
Just trust how it feels, though it does seem unreal
Your daddy was here, just ask the seal

DON'T STOP BREATHING

I watched you being there, you watched me disappear
Saw you full of fear, I wish I could wipe away that tear

As I witnessed the sense of sadness taking over from anger and fear
Only then could we try to accept that the end is near

But then I saw the tiniest leaf
Too small for me, but the perfect size for my soul
Carried around by the breath of loved ones
Carried by the breath of my precious girls

Down in the valley where the grass grows green
Is a place that nobody but me has seen
The walls are deep and dark and wide
I bet it's even better on the other side

I saw this leaf today, didn't quite know what to say
But it made me realise we had found the perfect size

It's up to you to help me through to a place where things are true
To a place where we believe that tiny leaves keep souls alive

I'm here but drifting away, only you can help me stay
Keep me in mind when times are tough, never forget the fun and love

I'll give you strength to carry on, you must believe I'm watching on
We'll be there dancing away in the kitchen like good old days

Once I'm through on my leaf I'll be there whenever you need me
It's up to you to help me through, it's up to you to keep me true

Don't stop breathing, don't stop breathing
Keep the leaf alive and keep belief in life

Down in the valley where the grass grows green
Is a place that nobody but me has seen

———

YOU CAN CALL ON ME

I am watching you from this field of grass
You can see me but you don't need me

I can see you talking but only hear myself
If you noticed me you'd run away

Yet I love you all and I watch you all
I am always here, guarding you

From a burning house or a falling tree
You can call on me, you can call on me

HOW LUCKY WE ARE

Oh, how lucky we are, Oh, how lucky we are,
Oh, how lucky we are, we got the sun and the rain
We've got the sun and the rain, the sun and the rain

I wish that everybody could see that
I wish that everybody could see
I wish that everybody could see that
And not drive themselves to death, for bigger cars and better things

Oh, how lucky we are, Oh, how lucky we are,
Oh, how lucky we are, we got the sun and the rain
We've got the sun and the rain, the sun and the rain

If only we appreciated each other instead of wanting to change
everyone
Expectations of other people are wrong, so wrong
We should see people, yeah people, we should see people as they are

Oh, how lucky we are, Oh, how lucky we are,
Oh, how lucky we are, we got the sun and the rain
We've got the sun and the rain, the sun and the rain

Defined by our achievements, what do you do?
What do you do?

SKIMMING ALONG

Skimming along, skimming along, skimming along over rainbows
Knocking so hard on the door of a spaceship wondering whether they
see me

Skimming along, skimming along, skimming along in the freedom of
space
But they are not skimming they are just sitting
Paying their way without skill or belief

Skimming through time I witnessed three star men
Who travelled this path from the earth to the moon
They floated through space without paying a penny
Risking their lives in pursuit of the truth

Fat cats have followed, cushioned from danger
By those who are skilled and have faith in themselves
Skimming back further I'll see the three wise men
Who followed a star

None of them saw me safe on my rainbow
Swinging my legs as I watched them
I'll skip through my rainbow the prisms of light
I'm free and I'm happy with wonderful views

Of the planet beneath me, the forests and pastures and oceans so blue

Marred by the cities where fat cats get richer
Where poor men survive without money or roof
Fighting for something that doesn't exist
Greedy for more and more's never enough

I'll settle for space and the beautiful rainbows
And the stars that surround me and hold me in truth

SONG FOR JAMES

On the day that you were born you came from darkness into light
How strange it must have been, how strange
I was pacing on the floor listening for the phone
To tell me you were here safe into the world

Safe into the world at last, safe into the world

From a baby to a boy, from a boy into a man
I have watched you grow, I've watched you fly, fly, fly, fly

And though I know that's how you dream
Your dreams can lead you home

SARA

Sara, October girl, Sara, October girl
Born after sunset, just as the harvest moon rose

Sara, October girl, mermaid without a tail
So cross at leaving the warm water place

In a hurry as she's always been
Two days early as I knew she'd be
And such an angry bunny

Sara, fearless child, Sara made up her mind
Race to the water, wherever it might be

What a funny girl
Such a faithful girl
Golden girl

Just a little tomboy climbing trees
Slipped out of windows when no one sees
Little miss adventure

Keeps on going when the going gets tough
Like Tina Turner when she struts her stuff
Those brown-eyed looks speak volumes

Caution comes with wisdom
You can't be brave if you have no fear, have no fear, Sara

Sara, October girl
New waters lie ahead

THE ANTIBIOTIC BLUES

Woke up this morning feeling like shit
Looked in the medicine cabinet decided to take a hit
Cus, baby, I got the antibiotic blues
Don't like feeling like this and the tragedy is
I can't take no more booze

Well there's Horlicks in the cupboard, and the cat is feeling rough
Ain't nothing I can do about it, I hate the rotten stuff
Cus, baby, I got the antibiotic blues
Don't like feeling like this and the tragedy is
I can't take no more booze

Double up on painkillers, paracetamol don't work
Ran out of codeine, baby, I'm going berserk

Well I ain't got no fix, like how I used to mix
I never took 'em one at a time, it was more like five or six
Cus, baby, I got the antibiotic blues
Don't like feeling like this and the tragedy is
I can't take no more booze

I used to take them all the time…with booze

GRACE

Winter is nearly over; I smell the breath of spring
New leaves are coming on the trees, they change every day

Repeat the patterns as new seasons grow
Roll us forward into bluer skies
Roll on in their never-ending circle
It lifts my heart as the days get longer

Grace, it's what I long for
Grace, it's what I've searched for
It never seemed to find me in the right place
So maybe you can be my saving grace

LUNCH

Some days you do, some days you don't
Some days you will and some days you won't
But your lunch is always waiting just the same

Some days you go, some days you stop
Some days you're high and some days you drop
And your lunch is getting dried up just the same

Some days the phone rings, some days not
Some days you catch up, but hey, not a lot
And your lunch is sitting spoiling just the same

Some days I wonder if I will starve
Some days my guts growl, it's terribly hard
But your lunch it gets more furry every hour

Here on the treadmill it's no fun
The walk of life's become a run

Forget about lunch, dream of tea
Home with the feet up, that'll do me
And your lunch is still there waiting just the same

HELLO TO YOU, MY DARLING

Hello to you, my darling, it's good to have you here
We have waited so long for you, now we can raise a cheer
Yes, we can raise a cheer

It's great to know you made it, one more baby in the land
We can watch you growing bigger and help you understand

Mum and Dad are there for you
Mum and Dad are there for you
Mum and Dad are there for you
A lucky baby, tell you true

Sister L sees your worth, loved you since before your birth
You can tell her when you're blue, she will weave a smile for you
She will weave a smile for you

No one will cause you pain, she will wash them down the drain
In all the things that you may do, she will take care of you
She will take care of you

Mum and Dad are there for you
Mum and Dad are there for you
Mum and Dad are there for you
A lucky baby, tell you true

Where does all this talking lead a guide to help you succeed
You've got family all around, you will float not run aground
You will float not run aground

Sun should always shine on you and on your sister girl times two
Take this world and if it snores, twist its tail until it roars
Twist its tail until it roars

Mum and Dad are there for you
Mum and Dad are there for you
Mum and Dad are there for you
A lucky baby, tell you true

Printed in Great Britain
by Amazon